CHINESE

COOKING for BEGINNERS

pil

Publications International, Ltd.

Photograph on front cover, page 75 and artwork on cover and pages 4, 5, 6 and 8 © Shutterstock.com.

Pictured on the front cover: Sesame Chili Beef (*page 74*).

Pictured on the back cover (clockwise from top left): Crab Rangoon with Spicy Dipping Sauce (*page 16*), Asian Baked Cod (*page 125*), Spicy Fried Rice with Tofu (*page 149*), and Hot and Sour Soup (*page 41*).

ISBN: 978-1-64558-642-5

Manufactured in China.

8 7 6 5 4 3 2 1

Microwave Cooking: Microwave ovens vary in wattage. Use the cooking times as guidelines and check for doneness before adding more time.

WARNING: Food preparation, baking and cooking involve inherent dangers: misuse of electric products, sharp electric tools, boiling water, hot stoves, allergic reactions, foodborne illnesses and the like, pose numerous potential risks. Publications International, Ltd. (PIL) assumes no responsibility or liability for any damages you may experience as a result of following recipes, instructions, tips or advice in this publication.

While we hope this publication helps you find new ways to eat delicious foods, you may not always achieve the results desired due to variations in ingredients, cooking temperatures, typos, errors, omissions, or individual cooking abilities.

Let's get social!

@Publications_International

@PublicationsInternational

www.pilbooks.com

CONTENTS

CHINESE
COOKING for BEGINNERS

It's not surprising that Chinese food is an American favorite. We may have started with egg rolls and chop suey in a little paper carton with a handle, but we've graduated to an appreciation to more authentic Chinese and Asian cuisines.

Chinese and Asian food fits with the way we eat now. It uses a little bit of meat or fish to add savor to a large amount of vegetables and rice—celebrating the freshness of vegetables and the rich, umami flavor of mushrooms and soy sauce.

Creating the distinctive flavors and contrasting textures of Asian cuisine in a home kitchen is less difficult than you would think. The recipes in this book use techniques and ingredients that will be mostly familiar to you. A few less mainstream products can usually be found in the Asian aisle of the supermarket, purchased online or found at a specialty store. Enjoy this collection of recipes from various regions of China, as well as a few Asian flavors you'll enjoy as well.

Many Chinese recipes are stir-fried. Organization is the key to success. There are often numerous ingredients that need to be cut into bite-size pieces before you start cooking. It's best to have small bowls lined up next to the stove holding individual ingredients so you won't waste time searching for something at the last minute.

You don't have to have a wok to stir-fry, but it just may be the most versatile cooking vessel ever invented. You can stir-fry, sauté, braise or deep-fry in a wok. It can also serve as a skillet, a soup pot or a steamer. There are many kinds of woks available, but an inexpensive carbon steel model, seasoned according to the manufacturer's instructions, works well. Beware of some nonstick-coated pans and electric woks. They can't get hot enough safely to handle real stir-fying. You can easily use a large deep skillet instead of a wok. Make sure that it can withstand high heat and that it is heavy enough to retain it. Rounded sides will make it easier to toss ingredients or remove them as needed.

Rice 101

Many Chinese and Asian meals include rice in some form. And, as a visit to any Asian market will prove, rice comes in many forms and varieties. The two most basic types are long grain and short grain. Long grain rice has slender grains that cook up relatively firm and fluffy. Short grain rice, which can be almost round, has an outer layer that absorbs water easily, so the cooked product is soft and a bit sticky. This is an advantage when you want to pick it up with chopsticks.

Arborio rice is short grain. Jasmine and basmati are examples of long grain varieties. Brown rice is any variety that has not been polished to remove the rice bran layer and the germ. It retains vitamins and fiber, but takes considerably longer to cook and is more perishable. White rice is preferred in Asian cuisines.

Secrets to Perfect Rice

1. Use Very Low Heat. If you don't have a burner that holds a low simmer, invest in a device called a heat diffuser or "flame tamer." This round, perforated metal disc rests right on the burner, under the saucepan, to keep the heat even.

2. Don't Peek! Once the saucepan is covered, don't open it until the cooking time is up. Even a small loss of heat can make a real difference.

3. Invest in a Rice Cooker. Most Asian cooks use one. Rice cookers not only turn out perfect rice every time, most will keep it warm for you, too.

Asian Noodles

Thick or thin, curly or flat, made of wheat, rice and even buckwheat, Asian noodles offer a continent's worth of flavors and textures to explore. Next time you want to turn vegetables into a meal, just start noodling around.

Chinese wheat noodles (mein) are similar to pasta and come in just as many styles and shapes with or without the addition of egg. They are cooked like pasta, so you can substitute a similar pasta shape if you have trouble finding the Asian version.

Rice noodles come in a dizzying array of sizes and go by a confusing number of names—rice sticks and rice vermicelli are two. Southeast Asian cooking uses rice noodles for many classic dishes. Unlike wheat noodles, rice noodles only need to be soaked in hot water before using.

Asian Noodles (continued)

Soba noodles are flat Japanese noodles made with buckwheat flour, which gives them an earthy, nutty flavor. They are served cold during Japanese summers and hot in winter soups. Soba should be cooked until tender, not al dente.

Udon noodles are thick, white Japanese or Korean noodles made from wheat flour and water. They are typically served in broth.

Asian Cooking Glossary

basil: Several varieties of basil are used in Asian cooking, including Thai basil, which has an anise-mint flavor and purple stems, and holy basil, which has a sharp, spicy-hot taste. Ordinary sweet basil is quite close in flavor to Thai basil and is a readily available substitute.

bean sprouts: The crisp, delicate sprouts of mung beans are extremely perishable. Purchase bean sprouts that have their buds attached and that smell and look fresh, not musty or slimy. Refrigerate sprouts and use within a few days.

black bean sauce/hot black bean sauce: Bean sauces are made from fermented black soybeans (sometimes called salted or dried black beans). Additional flavorings may include garlic, sugar and rice wine and, in the case of hot black bean sauce, chile peppers.

bok choy: The name bok choy means white vegetable and is a catch-all term for the many related Asian cabbages. Here the most common is the bok choy with green leaves and thick white stems. You will also find a smaller version labeled baby bok choy. The choy with green stems is often referred to as Shanghai choy. Almost all varieties are interchangeable and have similar flavors.

chile peppers: Both fresh and dried chile peppers are used. There are hundreds of varieties of fresh chiles. Jalapeño or serrano peppers are readily available and work well in Asian dishes. Dried red chile peppers are even hotter than fresh ones and can be slightly tamed by removing the seeds. In many recipes, dried red pepper flakes are called for instead of whole chiles as they are easier to find. Fresh or dried, care should be taken when handling chile peppers since they can sting and irritate the skin. Wear gloves when handling peppers and do not touch your eyes. Be sure to wash your hands and all surfaces and utensils that have been in contact with the peppers after handling.

coconut milk: Unsweetened canned coconut milk is available in the ethnic sections of most supermarkets. Do not confuse it with cream of coconut which is a sweetened product used in drinks like piña coladas. Nor is coconut milk the liquid inside a fresh coconut (that's coconut water). Coconut milk is made by combining water and the meat from a coconut, simmering and straining out solids.

chili garlic sauce or paste: This fiery combination of crushed red chiles and puréed garlic is available in many varieties and brands. The paste is more concentrated, so if you are substituting, use less.

curry pastes and powders: Most well-stocked supermarkets carry Thai red and green curry pastes in the Asian section. They can also be ordered online. They are made of chile peppers, lemongrass, shallots, garlic, ginger, coriander and cumin. Unless you're familiar with the product, always start by adding less curry paste than the recipe directs, since heat levels vary considerably from brand to brand. Curry powder comes in a variety of formulations as well. Indian curry powder is a mixture of as many as 20 different spices including chiles, cinnamon, cumin, fennel seeds, ginger, coriander and turmeric. Chinese and Southeast Asian curries may use their own different blends, but Madras curry powder is a good mainstream choice for all South Asian curries.

dashi: Used in miso soup and many other Japanese recipes, dashi is a stock or broth made with dried bonito (tuna) flakes and kelp.

five-spice powder: A mixture of ground cinnamon, cloves, fennel seeds, star anise and Szechuan peppercorns, five-spice powder is part of many Chinese dishes. It is said to include all five flavors—sweet, sour, salty, bitter and pungent.

fish sauce: This condiment is used in Southeast Asian cooking as soy sauce is in Chinese cuisine. Don't be put off by its funky aroma, which diminishes with cooking. Fish sauce helps balance and complete many dishes. It is possible to substitute soy sauce, but the results will be different.

ginger, fresh: Fresh ginger is the rhizome (an underground stem) of the ginger plant. It's a knobby, bumpy, beige root that you will find in the produce section. Ground ginger comes from the same plant, but has a different flavor.

ginger, pickled: These thin slices of fresh ginger are preserved in a vinegar pickling solution and served with sushi or used as a garnish in Japanese cuisine.

hoisin sauce: This thick reddish-brown sauce is sweet, salty and a bit spicy. It contains soybeans, chile peppers and various spices and is used in Peking duck along with other classic barbecue dishes.

lemongrass: The flowery perfume of lemongrass is one of the most delightful elements of Thai cooking. Minced finely, lemongrass is part of many curry pastes. The stalks are also cut into large pieces and used to flavor foods, rather like a bay leaf, then removed before serving. To use fresh lemongrass, cut off the moist portion at the root end. Throw away the dry, fibrous stalk and the outer leaves. The tender white portion may then be minced and used. Lemongrass freezes well. Grated lemon peel may be substituted, but with a substantial difference in flavor.

mirin: Mirin is a very sweet golden wine used in many Japanese sauces, marinades and glazes. It is not usually consumed as a beverage.

miso: This fermented, soy-based seasoning paste has a smooth, buttery texture and a tangy, salty taste. Miso is most commonly used in soup, but it is also used in dressings, marinades and sauces.

nori: These paper-thin sheets of seaweed are dry and dark greenish-black. Most nori is used to wrap sushi and is pre-toasted (yaki-nori). It can also be crumbled over rice or added to salads.

oyster sauce: A rich-tasting, dark brown sauce made from oysters, soy sauce and often MSG. Check the label to see if the sauce you're purchasing contains real oyster extract or just oyster flavoring.

rice noodles: These semi-translucent dried noodles come in many sizes and have many names, including rice stick noodles, rice-flour noodles and pho noodles. Widths range from string thin (usually called rice

vermicelli) to 1 inch wide. All rice noodles must be soaked or boiled before using and all may be used interchangeably provided soaking and cooking times are adjusted.

rice papers: Look for packages containing stacks of thin translucent rounds, 6 to 8 inches in diameter, in Asian markets. Rice papers look incredibly fragile but are actually fairly easy to handle. After soaking they become soft, flexible and a bit stretchy.

rice vinegar: Both Chinese and Japanese rice vinegars are made from fermented glutinous (sweet) rice. They are milder than regular white vinegars and also have a bit of sweetness. Seasoned rice vinegar has salt and sugar added and is used to flavor sushi rice.

rice wine: This slightly sweet wine is made from fermented glutinous rice. Shaoxing rice wine is a good variety. Avoid those labeled "cooking wine," since they often have salt or sugar added.

shiitake mushrooms: Shiitakes can be purchased fresh or dried. The dried ones are often simply called Chinese black mushrooms. The meaty texture and flavor of shiitakes works well in many preparations. The stems of shiitakes are woody and tough. Discard them or save them for flavoring soup or stock.

soy sauce: The quality of soy sauce can vary greatly. It is made from soybeans and roasted grain (usually wheat). Look for sauce that is naturally brewed. Cheaper soy sauce is often manufactured from hydrolyzed vegetable protein with corn syrup and color added. Regular soy sauce is sometimes referred to as light soy sauce and is the commonly available variety (not to be confused with reduced-sodium or "lite" soy). Dark soy sauce is brewed longer and is thicker and sweeter.

sushi rice: Rice prepared for sushi is the short-grain variety. It is boiled, then quickly cooled and dressed with seasoned rice vinegar. If you can't find a product labeled "sushi rice," use another short-grain white rice.

straw mushrooms: Traditionally grown on straw used in rice paddies, straw mushrooms are available in cans in Asian markets. They are sometimes labeled "peeled" or "unpeeled," which refers to whether or not the caps have opened. Rinse carefully and drain straw mushrooms before using them.

Szechuan pepper/peppercorns: This mildly hot spice is no relation to black peppercorns or chile peppers. It has a slightly flowery, lemony flavor and aroma and a unique tongue-numbing effect. Szechuan peppercorns are sometimes available in powdered form, but whole peppercorns are most often crushed right before using to release their flavor.

tamari: A Japanese version of soy sauce, tamari has a slightly thicker consistency and a stronger but mellower flavor. It is brewed like soy sauce, but usually does not contain wheat, which is an advantage for those who are sensitive to gluten.

tofu: Versatile tofu, also called bean curd, is a custard-like cake pressed from cooked ground soybeans. You can purchase it in soft, firm or extra-firm styles. Bland by itself, tofu readily takes on the flavors of whatever it is cooked with. It is low in calories, high in protein and cholesterol free.

wasabi: This bright green condiment is sold in the form of a powder, which must be reconstituted with water, or a paste. It's known as Japanese horseradish because it has the same powerful, sinus-clearing flavor.

wonton wrappers: Sometimes called wonton skins, these extremely thin sheets of dough are made of flour and water. In supermarkets, they are usually found in the refrigerated section near tofu. A 12-ounce package contains 4 or 5 dozen wrappers.

APPETIZERS & DIM SUM

SWEET-HOT ORANGE CHICKEN DRUMETTES

Makes about 5 servings

¼ **cup plus 3 tablespoons orange juice, divided**

4 **tablespoons orange marmalade or apricot jam, divided**

3 **tablespoons hoisin sauce**

1 **teaspoon grated fresh ginger**

10 **chicken drumettes (about 1¼ pounds)**

3 **tablespoons chili garlic sauce**

¼ **teaspoon salt**

¼ **teaspoon red pepper flakes**

⅛ **teaspoon Chinese five-spice powder (optional)**

⅛ **teaspoon black pepper**

Sesame seeds (optional)

1. Preheat oven to 400°F. Line baking sheet with heavy-duty foil; generously spray foil with nonstick cooking spray.

2. Combine ¼ cup orange juice, 2 tablespoons orange marmalade, hoisin sauce and ginger in medium microwavable bowl. Microwave on HIGH 1 minute or until marmalade melts; stir until well blended. Dip drumettes, one at a time, in orange juice mixture; place on prepared baking sheet.

3. Bake 15 minutes; turn and bake 5 to 10 minutes or until drumettes are golden brown and cooked through.

4. Meanwhile, combine remaining 3 tablespoons orange juice, 2 tablespoons orange marmalade, chili garlic sauce, salt, red pepper flakes, five-spice powder, if desired, and black pepper in small microwavable bowl. Microwave on HIGH 1 minute or until marmalade melts; stir until well blended.

5. Sprinkle drumettes with sesame seeds; serve with dipping sauce.

BAKED PORK BUNS

Makes 20 buns

1 tablespoon vegetable oil

2 cups coarsely chopped bok choy

1 small onion or large shallot, thinly sliced

1 container (18 ounces) refrigerated shredded barbecue pork

All-purpose flour

2 packages (10 ounces each) refrigerated jumbo buttermilk biscuits (5 biscuits per package)

1. Preheat oven to 350°F. Line baking sheet with parchment paper or spray with nonstick cooking spray.

2. Heat oil in large skillet over medium-high heat. Add bok choy and onion; cook and stir 8 to 10 minutes or until vegetables are tender. Remove from heat; stir in barbecue pork.

3. Lightly flour work surface. Separate biscuits; split each biscuit in half to create two thin biscuits. Roll each biscuit half into 5-inch circle.

4. Spoon heaping tablespoon pork mixture onto one side of each circle. Fold dough over filling to form half circle; press edges to seal. Place buns on prepared baking sheet.

5. Bake 12 to 15 minutes or until golden brown.

FAN-TAILED CHINESE SHRIMP

Makes 6 servings

- 1 tablespoon seasoned rice vinegar
- 1 tablespoon oyster sauce
- 1 tablespoon soy sauce
- 2 cloves garlic, minced
- ¼ teaspoon red pepper flakes
- 18 large raw shrimp (about 1 pound), peeled and deveined (with tails on)
- 1 tablespoon peanut or canola oil
- ¼ cup chopped fresh cilantro

  Prepared plum sauce or sweet and sour sauce (optional)

1. Combine vinegar, oyster sauce, soy sauce, garlic and red pepper flakes in large bowl until well blended.

2. To butterfly shrimp, use small sharp knife to cut each shrimp down back (where vein was) three fourths of the way through shrimp. Open shrimp; place cut side down on work surface, pressing to flatten into butterfly shape. Add shrimp to bowl with marinade; toss gently to coat. Cover and refrigerate at least 30 minutes or up to 2 hours.

3. Heat oil in large nonstick skillet over medium heat. Remove shrimp from marinade; discard marinade. Cook shrimp in batches 3 to 4 minutes or until pink and opaque, turning once. Remove to serving platter; sprinkle with cilantro. Serve with plum sauce for dipping, if desired.

CRAB RANGOON
with SPICY DIPPING SAUCE

Makes about 12 servings (44 wontons)

Dipping Sauce

- **1 cup ketchup**
- **¼ cup chili garlic sauce**
- **4 teaspoons Chinese hot mustard**

Crab Rangoon

- **1 package (8 ounces) cream cheese, softened**
- **1 can (6 ounces) lump crabmeat, well drained**
- **⅓ cup minced green onions**
- **1 package (12 ounces) wonton wrappers**
- **1 egg white, beaten**
- **Vegetable oil for frying**

1. Combine ketchup, chili garlic sauce and mustard in small bowl; mix well.

2. Beat cream cheese in medium bowl with electric mixer at medium speed until light and fluffy. Stir in crabmeat and green onions.

3. Arrange wonton wrappers, one at a time, on clean work surface. Place 1 rounded teaspoon crab mixture in center of wrapper. Brush inside edges of wonton wrapper with egg white. Fold wonton diagonally in half to form triangle;* press edges firmly to seal.

4. Pour oil into deep heavy saucepan to depth of 2 inches; heat to 350°F over medium-high heat. Fry wontons in batches 2 minutes per side or until golden brown. Remove with slotted spoon to paper towel-lined plate. Serve immediately with dipping sauce.

*Wonton wrappers are not quite square so they will not form perfect triangles.

Variation: Crab Rangoon can be baked instead of fried, but the results will not be as crisp or as golden in color. Prepare as directed through step 3, then arrange triangles 1 inch apart on parchment-lined baking sheets. Spray tops of triangles with nonstick cooking spray. Bake in preheated 375°F oven about 11 minutes or until lightly browned. Serve immediately.

STEAMED PORK WONTONS
with SWEET SOY DIPPING SAUCE

Makes 8 servings

Wontons

- **8 ounces lean ground pork**
- **¼ cup chopped fresh cilantro**
- **1½ tablespoons grated fresh ginger**
- **1 teaspoon grated orange peel**
- **¼ teaspoon ground red pepper**
- **⅛ teaspoon salt**
- **24 wonton wrappers**
- **3 teaspoons vegetable oil, divided**
- **1 cup water, divided**

Dipping Sauce

- **2 to 3 tablespoons pourable sugar substitute***
- **2 tablespoons white vinegar**
- **2 tablespoons lime juice**
- **2 tablespoons reduced-sodium soy sauce**

  *This recipe was tested using sucralose-based sugar substitute.

1. Combine pork, cilantro, ginger, orange peel, red pepper and salt in medium bowl; mix well. Working with one wonton wrapper at a time, place rounded teaspoon pork mixture in center of wrapper. Moisten edges with water and bring corners together; twist to seal.

2. Heat 1½ teaspoons oil in large nonstick skillet over medium-high heat. Add 12 wontons; cook 1 minute or until bottoms are golden brown. Add ½ cup water; cover and cook 5 minutes or until water has evaporated. Remove to platter; tent with foil to keep warm. Repeat with remaining oil, wontons and water.

3. Combine sauce ingredients in small bowl until well blended. If desired, microwave on HIGH 20 to 30 seconds. Serve with wontons.

DIM SUM RAVIOLI

Makes 4 servings

¼ cup plain dry bread crumbs

½ teaspoon dried parsley flakes

¼ teaspoon garlic powder

36 uncooked small cheese ravioli

1 cup water

2 tablespoons sugar

2 tablespoons rice wine vinegar

1 tablespoon cornstarch

1 tablespoon reduced-sodium soy sauce

1 teaspoon grated fresh ginger

½ teaspoon dark sesame oil

⅓ cup minced fresh cilantro

1. Preheat oven to 350°F. Combine bread crumbs, parsley flakes and garlic powder in small bowl; set aside.

2. Cook ravioli according to package directions, omitting salt. Drain.

3. Spray each ravioli with nonstick cooking spray and place on cookie sheet. Sprinkle with bread crumb mixture. Spray several times with cooking spray. Bake, uncovered, 3 to 5 minutes or until golden brown.

4. Bring water to a boil in small saucepan over high heat. Reduce heat to medium; add sugar. Cook 30 seconds or until sugar is dissolved. Add vinegar; cook 1 minute.

5. Combine cornstarch and soy sauce in small bowl. Add to sugar-vinegar mixture, stirring constantly, 1 to 2 minutes or until slightly thickened. Remove from heat. Stir in ginger, sesame oil and cilantro. Serve sauce in bowls for dipping.

FRIED TOFU
with SESAME DIPPING SAUCE

Makes 4 servings

3 tablespoons soy sauce or tamari

2 tablespoons unseasoned rice vinegar

2 teaspoons sugar

1 teaspoon sesame seeds, toasted*

1 teaspoon dark sesame oil

⅛ teaspoon red pepper flakes

1 package (about 14 ounces) extra firm tofu

2 tablespoons all-purpose flour

1 egg

¾ cup panko bread crumbs

4 tablespoons vegetable oil

*To toast sesame seeds, spread seeds in small skillet. Shake skillet over medium-low heat about 3 minutes or until seeds begin to pop and turn golden.

1. Whisk soy sauce, vinegar, sugar, sesame seeds, sesame oil and red pepper flakes in small bowl until well blended; set aside.

2. Drain tofu and press between paper towels to remove excess water. Cut crosswise into four slices; cut each slice diagonally into triangles. Place flour in shallow dish. Beat egg in shallow bowl. Place panko in another shallow bowl.

3. Dip each piece of tofu in flour, turning to lightly coat all sides. Dip in egg, letting excess drip back into bowl. Roll in panko to coat.

4. Heat 2 tablespoons vegetable oil in large nonstick skillet over high heat. Reduce heat to medium; add half of tofu in single layer. Cook 1 to 2 minutes per side or until golden brown. Repeat with remaining tofu. Serve with sauce for dipping.

BAKED EGG ROLLS

Makes 6 servings

Sesame Dipping Sauce (recipe follows)

1 ounce dried shiitake mushrooms

1 large carrot, shredded

1 can (8 ounces) sliced water chestnuts, drained and minced

3 green onions, minced

3 tablespoons chopped fresh cilantro

12 ounces ground chicken

2 tablespoons minced fresh ginger

6 cloves garlic, minced

2 tablespoons reduced-sodium soy sauce

2 teaspoons water

1 teaspoon cornstarch

12 wonton wrappers

1 tablespoon vegetable oil

1 teaspoon sesame seeds

1. Prepare Sesame Dipping Sauce; set aside.

2. Place mushrooms in small bowl. Cover with warm water; let stand 30 minutes or until tender. Rinse well; drain, squeezing out excess water. Cut off and discard stems; finely chop caps. Combine mushrooms, carrot, water chestnuts, green onions and cilantro in large bowl.

3. Spray medium nonstick skillet with nonstick cooking spray; heat over medium-high heat. Brown chicken 2 minutes, stirring to break up meat. Add ginger and garlic; cook and stir 2 minutes or until chicken is cooked through. Add to mushroom mixture. Sprinkle with soy sauce; mix thoroughly.

4. Preheat oven to 425°F. Spray baking sheet with cooking spray; set aside. Stir 2 teaspoons water into cornstarch in small bowl. Lay 1 wonton wrapper on work surface. Spoon about ⅓ cup filling across center of wrapper to within about ½ inch of sides. Fold bottom of wrapper over filling. Fold in sides. Brush ½-inch strip across top edge with cornstarch mixture; roll up and seal securely. Place seam side down on baking sheet. Repeat with remaining wrappers.

5. Brush egg rolls with oil. Sprinkle with sesame seeds. Bake 18 minutes or until golden and crisp. Serve with Sesame Dipping Sauce.

SESAME DIPPING SAUCE

Makes about ½ cup

¼ **cup rice vinegar**

4 **teaspoons reduced-sodium soy sauce**

2 **teaspoons minced fresh ginger**

1 **teaspoon dark sesame oil**

Combine all ingredients in small bowl; blend well.

SHRIMP TOAST

Makes 12 servings (1 dozen appetizers)

12 large raw shrimp, peeled
    and deveined (with tails
    on)

 1 egg

2½ tablespoons cornstarch

 ¼ teaspoon salt

    Dash black pepper

 3 slices white sandwich
    bread, each cut into
    4 triangles

 1 slice (1 ounce) cooked ham,
    cut into ½-inch pieces

    Vegetable oil for frying

 2 hard-cooked egg yolks,
    chopped

 1 green onion, finely chopped

1. Cut deep slit down back of each shrimp; press gently with fingers to flatten.

2. Beat egg, cornstarch, salt and pepper in large bowl until blended. Add shrimp; toss to coat.

3. Drain each shrimp and press, cut side down, onto each piece of bread. Brush small amount of remaining egg mixture onto each shrimp. Place piece of ham on top of each shrimp, pressing to adhere.

4. Heat about 1 inch oil to 375°F in wok or large skillet over medium-high heat. Add 3 or 4 bread pieces to wok at a time; cook 1 to 2 minutes or until cooked through and toast is golden brown, spooning hot oil over shrimp. Drain on paper towel-lined plate. Sprinkle with egg yolk and green onion.

DIM SUM BAKED BUNS

Makes 16 buns

6 **to 8 dried shiitake mushrooms**

3 **green onions, minced**

2 **tablespoons prepared plum sauce**

1 **tablespoon hoisin sauce**

8 **ounces ground chicken**

4 **cloves garlic, minced**

1 **tablespoon minced fresh ginger**

8 **frozen bread dough rolls (about 18 ounces), thawed according to package directions**

2 **tablespoons cholesterol-free egg substitute**

¾ **teaspoon sesame seeds**

1. Place mushrooms in medium bowl. Cover with warm water; let stand 30 minutes. Line two baking sheets with parchment paper or spray with nonstick cooking spray.

2. Rinse mushrooms and drain, squeezing out excess water. Cut off and discard stems. Finely chop caps; return to bowl. Add green onions, plum sauce and hoisin sauce.

3. Spray medium nonstick skillet with cooking spray; heat over high heat. Add chicken; cook, without stirring, 1 to 2 minutes or until no longer pink. Add garlic and ginger; cook and stir 2 minutes. Stir in mushroom mixture.

4. Lightly flour hands and work surface. Cut rolls in half; roll each half into a ball. Shape each piece between hands to form disk. Press edge of disk between thumb and forefinger, working in circular motion to form circle 3 to 3½ inches in diameter (center of disk should be thicker than edges.)

5. Place disks on work surface. Place 1 generous tablespoon filling in center of each disk. Lift edge of dough up and around filling; pinch edges together to seal. Place seam side down on prepared baking sheets. Cover with towel; let rise in warm place 45 minutes or until doubled in size. Preheat oven to 375°F.

6. Brush buns with egg substitute; sprinkle evenly with sesame seeds. Bake 16 to 18 minutes or until golden brown.

EGG FOO YUNG

Makes 4 servings

2 eggs

2 egg whites

½ cup fresh or canned bean sprouts, rinsed and drained

½ cup chopped fresh mushrooms

2 tablespoons thinly sliced green onion

2 tablespoons soy sauce, divided

1 tablespoon peanut or vegetable oil

1 cup chicken broth

1 tablespoon cornstarch

¼ teaspoon sugar

¼ teaspoon black pepper

1. Beat eggs and egg whites in large bowl. Stir in bean sprouts, mushrooms, green onion and 1 tablespoon soy sauce.

2. Heat oil in large nonstick skillet over medium-high heat. Pour ¼ cupfuls egg mixture into skillet (egg mixture will run; do not crowd skillet). Cook 1 to 2 minutes or until bottoms are set. Turn over; cook 1 to 2 minutes or until cooked through. Remove to large plate; keep warm. Repeat with remaining egg mixture.

3. Whisk broth, remaining 1 tablespoon soy sauce and cornstarch in small bowl until smooth and well blended; add to skillet. Stir in sugar and pepper; cook and stir 1 minute or until sauce boils and is thickened. Pour sauce over warm pancakes; serve immediately.

Variation: Add ½ cup chopped cooked shrimp or ½ cup diced roasted pork to egg mixture.

SHRIMP DUMPLINGS with BLACK BEAN COFFEE SAUCE

Makes about 3 dozen dumplings

Dumplings

- ½ **pound medium shrimp, peeled and deveined**
- 1 **teaspoon grated fresh ginger**
- 2 **green onions, thinly sliced**
- 1 **tablespoon reduced-sodium soy sauce**
- 1 **teaspoon dark sesame oil**
- 1 **can (5 ounces) water chestnuts, drained and chopped**
- 1 **can (5 ounces) bamboo shoots, drained and chopped**
- ¼ **cup fresh cilantro**
- ¼ **cup fresh basil**
- 1 **package (1.5 ounces) wonton wrappers**
- 3 **tablespoons cold water**

Sauce

- 1 **teaspoon dark sesame oil**
- 4 **tablespoons bottled black bean with garlic sauce**
- ½ **cup brewed coffee**
- ½ **teaspoon hoisin sauce**

1. Pulse shrimp, ginger, green onions, soy sauce and 1 teaspoon oil in food processor until paste forms. Add water chestnuts, bamboo shoots, cilantro and basil; pulse briefly.

2. Place 40 wonton wrappers on work surface lined with wax or parchment paper. Using small brush, moisten edges of wrappers with cold water. Place 1 heaping teaspoon shrimp mixture into center of each wrapper. Fold wrapper over filling to form triangle; press edges to seal.

3. Place steamer insert into small pot. Pour water into pot to just below steamer. Spray steamer with nonstick cooking spray. Bring water to a boil.

4. Place dumplings in steamer (allow space between each dumpling). Cover; steam about 8 minutes or until filling is cooked and dough is shiny and translucent.

5. To make sauce, heat 1 teaspoon sesame oil in medium skillet. Add black bean sauce, coffee and hoisin sauce; stir until combined. Remove from heat, cover and keep warm.

6. Serve hot dumplings with warm sauce for dipping.

POT STICKERS

Makes about 3 dozen

- **2 cups all-purpose flour, plus additional for work surface**
- **¾ cup plus 2 tablespoons boiling water**
- **½ cup very finely chopped napa cabbage**
- **8 ounces lean ground pork**
- **2 tablespoons finely chopped water chestnuts**
- **1 green onion, finely chopped**
- **1½ teaspoons dry sherry**
- **1½ teaspoons soy sauce**
- **1½ teaspoons cornstarch**
- **½ teaspoon minced fresh ginger**
- **½ teaspoon dark sesame oil**
- **¼ teaspoon sugar**
- **2 tablespoons vegetable oil, divided**
- **⅔ cup chicken broth, divided**
- **Soy sauce, vinegar and chili oil**

1. Place 2 cups flour in large bowl; make well in center. Pour in boiling water; stir with wooden spoon until dough forms.

2. On lightly floured surface, knead dough about 5 minutes or until smooth and satiny. Cover dough; let rest 30 minutes.

3. For filling, squeeze cabbage to remove as much moisture as possible; place in large bowl. Add pork, water chestnuts, green onion, sherry, soy sauce, cornstarch, ginger, sesame oil and sugar; mix well.

4. Divide dough into two equal portions; cover one portion with plastic wrap or clean towel while working with other portion. On lightly floured surface, roll out dough to ⅛-inch thickness. Cut out 3-inch circles with round cookie cutter or top of clean empty can.

5. Place 1 rounded teaspoon filling in center of each dough circle.

6. To shape each pot sticker, lightly moisten edges of one dough circle with water; fold in half. Starting at one end, pinch edges together making four pleats along edge; set dumpling down firmly, seam side up. Cover finished dumplings while shaping remaining dumplings. (Dumplings may be refrigerated for up to 4 hours or frozen in large resealable food storage bag.)

7. To cook dumplings, heat 1 tablespoon vegetable oil in large nonstick skillet over medium heat. Place half of pot stickers in skillet, seam side up. (If cooking frozen dumplings, do not thaw.) Cook 5 to 6 minutes or until bottoms are golden brown.

8. Pour in ⅓ cup broth; cover tightly. Reduce heat to low. Simmer until all liquid is absorbed, about 10 minutes (15 minutes if frozen). Repeat with remaining vegetable oil, dumplings and broth.

9. Serve with soy sauce, vinegar and chili oil for dipping.

SZECHUAN GRILLED MUSHROOMS

Makes 4 servings

1 **pound large mushrooms**

2 **tablespoons soy sauce**

2 **teaspoons peanut or vegetable oil**

1 **teaspoon dark sesame oil**

1 **clove garlic, minced**

½ **teaspoon crushed Szechuan peppercorns or red pepper flakes**

1. Place mushrooms in large resealable food storage bag. Combine soy sauce, peanut oil, sesame oil, garlic and Szechuan peppercorns in small bowl; pour over mushrooms. Seal bag; turn to coat. Marinate at room temperature 15 minutes.

2. Prepare grill for direct cooking. Thread mushrooms onto skewers.*

3. Grill or broil mushrooms 5 inches from heat 10 minutes or until lightly browned, turning once. Serve immediately.

*If using wooden skewers, soak 20 minutes in cool water before threading with food.

Variation: For Szechuan-Grilled Mushrooms and Onions, add 4 green onions, cut into 1½-inch pieces, to marinade. Alternately thread onto skewers with mushrooms. Proceed as directed in step 2.

SCALLION PANCAKES

Makes 32 wedges

2 cups all-purpose flour,
  plus additional for work
  surface

1 teaspoon sugar

⅔ cup boiling water

¼ to ½ cup cold water

2 teaspoons dark sesame oil

½ cup finely chopped green
  onion tops

1 teaspoon coarse salt

½ to ¾ cup vegetable oil

1. Combine 2 cups flour and sugar in large bowl. Stir in boiling water; mix with fork just until water is absorbed and mixture forms large clumps. Gradually stir in cold water until dough forms a ball and is no longer sticky.

2. Place dough on lightly floured surface; flatten slightly. Knead dough 5 minutes or until smooth and elastic. Wrap dough with plastic wrap; let stand 1 hour.

3. Unwrap dough and knead briefly on lightly floured surface; divide dough into four pieces. Roll one piece into 6- to 7-inch round, keeping remaining pieces wrapped in plastic wrap to prevent drying out. Brush dough with ½ teaspoon sesame oil; sprinkle evenly with 2 tablespoons green onions and ¼ teaspoon salt. Roll up jelly-roll fashion into tight cylinder.

4. Coil cylinder into a spiral and pinch end under into dough. Repeat with remaining dough pieces, sesame oil, green onions and salt. Cover with plastic wrap and let stand 15 minutes.

5. Roll each coiled piece of dough into 6- to 7-inch round on lightly floured surface with floured rolling pin.

6. Heat ½ cup vegetable oil in wok over medium-high heat to 375°F on deep-fry thermometer. Carefully place one pancake into hot oil. Fry 2 to 3 minutes per side or until golden. While pancake is frying, press center lightly with metal spatula to ensure even cooking. Remove to paper towels to drain. Repeat with remaining pancakes, adding additional oil if necessary.

7. Cut each pancake into eight wedges. Arrange on serving platter. Serve immediately.

SALADS & SOUPS

HOT and SOUR SOUP

Makes 7 servings

- **3 cans (about 14 ounces each) chicken broth**
- **8 ounces boneless skinless chicken breasts, cut into ¼-inch-thick strips**
- **1 cup shredded carrots**
- **1 cup thinly sliced mushrooms**
- **½ cup bamboo shoots, cut into matchstick-size strips**
- **2 tablespoons rice vinegar or white wine vinegar**
- **½ to ¾ teaspoon white pepper**
- **¼ to ½ teaspoon hot pepper sauce**
- **2 tablespoons cornstarch**
- **2 tablespoons soy sauce**
- **1 tablespoon dry sherry**
- **2 medium green onions, sliced**
- **1 egg, lightly beaten**

1. Combine broth, chicken, carrots, mushrooms, bamboo shoots, vinegar, white pepper and hot pepper sauce in large saucepan. Bring to a boil over medium-high heat; reduce heat to low. Cover and simmer about 5 minutes or until chicken is no longer pink.

2. Stir together cornstarch, soy sauce and sherry in small bowl until smooth. Add to broth mixture. Cook and stir until mixture comes to a boil. Stir in green onions and egg. Cook about 1 minute, stirring in one direction, until egg is cooked.

CHINESE CHICKEN SALAD

Makes 4 servings

4 cups chopped bok choy

3 cups diced cooked chicken breast

1 cup shredded carrots

2 tablespoons minced fresh chives or green onions

2 tablespoons hot chile sauce with garlic

1½ tablespoons peanut or canola oil

1 tablespoon balsamic vinegar

1 tablespoon soy sauce

1 teaspoon minced fresh ginger

1. Place bok choy, chicken, carrots and chives in large bowl.

2. Combine chile garlic sauce, oil, vinegar, soy sauce and ginger in small bowl; mix well. Pour over chicken mixture; toss gently.

SPINACH NOODLE BOWL with GINGER

Makes 4 servings

- **1** container (48 ounces) chicken broth
- **4** ounces uncooked vermicelli noodles, broken into thirds
- **1½** cups matchstick carrots
- **3** ounces snow peas, stemmed and cut into halves
- **4** cups packed stemmed fresh spinach (4 ounces)
- **1½** cups cooked shrimp or chicken
- **½** cup finely chopped green onions
- **1** tablespoon grated fresh ginger
- **1** teaspoon soy sauce
- **⅛** to ¼ teaspoon red pepper flakes

1. Bring broth to a boil in large saucepan or Dutch oven over high heat. Add noodles; return to a boil. Cook until al dente (about 2 minutes less than package directions). Add carrots and snow peas; cook 2 minutes or until noodles are tender.

2. Remove from heat; stir in spinach, shrimp, green onions, ginger, soy sauce and red pepper flakes. Let stand 2 minutes before serving.

ASIAN TOFU SALAD

Makes 5 servings

½ **package (16 ounces) extra-firm tofu, drained**

4 **tablespoons rice vinegar**

3 **tablespoons reduced-sodium soy sauce**

1½ **tablespoons sugar**

1 **tablespoon dark sesame oil or canola oil**

1 **to 2 teaspoons chili garlic sauce**

1 **teaspoon grated ginger**

1 **cup snow peas, trimmed**

8 **cups mixed salad greens**

2 **medium carrots, julienned**

1 **medium cucumber, thinly sliced**

¼ **cup unsalted dry roasted peanuts, coarsely chopped (optional)**

1. Cut tofu into ½-inch cubes, place in single layer on kitchen towel.

2. Mix vinegar, soy sauce, sugar, sesame oil, chili garlic sauce and ginger in small bowl.

3. Heat nonstick skillet over medium-high heat; add tofu, 2 tablespoons sauce mixture and snow peas. Cook and stir 5 to 7 minutes. Let cool slightly.

4. Place mixed greens in salad bowl and add carrots and cucumber. Drizzle with remaining sauce mixture and toss to mix.

5. Add warm tofu mixture and peanuts, if desired. Serve immediately.

ASIAN CHICKEN and SPINACH SALAD

Makes 4 servings

⅓ cup peanut oil

¼ cup honey

¼ cup soy sauce

2 teaspoons Worcestershire sauce

1 teaspoon dark sesame oil

3 boneless skinless chicken breasts (about 12 ounces), cut into 2-inch strips

1 cup baby carrots, cut crosswise into ¼-inch slices

3 cups coarsely chopped bok choy (stems and leaves)

3 cups spinach, torn into bite-size pieces

1 cup canned bean sprouts

¼ cup dry roasted peanuts

1. To prepare dressing, combine peanut oil, honey, soy sauce, Worcestershire sauce and sesame oil in small bowl; whisk until well blended.

2. Heat 2 tablespoons dressing in large nonstick skillet over medium heat. Add chicken and carrots; cook and stir about 5 minutes or until chicken is cooked through. Remove from skillet and let cool.

3. Heat another 2 tablespoons dressing in same skillet. Add bok choy; cook and stir about 1 minute or just until wilted.

4. Place spinach on individual plates. Arrange bok choy over spinach. Top with chicken, carrots and bean sprouts. Sprinkle with peanuts; serve with remaining dressing.

SZECHUAN CHICKEN SALAD
with PEANUT DRESSING

Makes 4 servings

1 **pound boneless skinless chicken breasts**

1 **can (about 14 ounces) chicken broth**

1 **tablespoon creamy peanut butter**

1 **tablespoon peanut or vegetable oil**

1 **tablespoon soy sauce**

1 **tablespoon rice vinegar**

1 **teaspoon dark sesame oil**

¼ **teaspoon ground red pepper**

Shredded lettuce

Chopped fresh cilantro or green onions (optional)

1. Place chicken in single layer in large skillet. Pour broth over chicken; bring to a boil over high heat. Reduce heat to medium-low. Cover; simmer 10 to 12 minutes or until chicken is no longer pink in center.

2. Meanwhile, mix peanut butter and peanut oil in small bowl until smooth. Stir in soy sauce, vinegar, sesame oil and red pepper.

3. Drain chicken, reserving 2 tablespoons broth.* Set chicken aside to cool. Slice, shred or coarsely chop cooled chicken.

4. Stir reserved broth into peanut butter mixture.

5. Arrange chicken on lettuce-lined plates. Serve salad with peanut dressing, and sprinkle with cilantro, if desired.

*Strain remaining broth; cover and refrigerate or freeze for use in other recipes.

WONTON SOUP

Makes 4 servings

- **4** ounces ground pork, chicken or turkey
- **¼** cup finely chopped water chestnuts
- **2** tablespoons soy sauce, divided
- **1** egg white, lightly beaten
- **1** teaspoon minced fresh ginger
- **12** wonton wrappers
- **6** cups chicken broth
- **1½** cups fresh spinach leaves, torn
- **1** cup thinly sliced cooked pork (optional)
- **½** cup diagonally sliced green onions
- **1** tablespoon dark sesame oil
  Shredded carrot (optional)

1. Combine ground pork, water chestnuts, 1 tablespoon soy sauce, egg white and ginger in small bowl; mix well.

2. Arrange wonton wrappers on clean work surface. Spoon 1 teaspoon filling near bottom point. Fold bottom point of wrapper up over filling; fold side points over filling. Moisten inside edges with water; bring edges together firmly to seal. Repeat with remaining wrappers and filling.* Keep finished wontons covered with plastic wrap while filling remaining wrappers.

3. Combine broth and remaining 1 tablespoon soy sauce in large saucepan; bring to a boil over high heat. Reduce heat to medium; add wontons. Simmer 4 minutes or until filling is cooked through.

4. Stir in spinach, sliced pork, if desired, and green onions; remove from heat. Stir in oil. Ladle soup into bowls; garnish with shredded carrot.

*Wontons may be made ahead to this point; cover and refrigerate up to 8 hours or freeze up to 3 months. Proceed as directed above if using refrigerated wontons; increase simmering time to 6 minutes if using frozen wontons.

CHINESE SALAD SUPREME

Makes 4 servings

¼ cup peanut or vegetable oil

¼ cup rice wine vinegar

2 tablespoons packed brown sugar

1 medium unpeeled cucumber, halved lengthwise and sliced

6 cups torn romaine or leaf lettuce

1 cup chow mein noodles

¼ cup peanuts or coarsely chopped cashew nuts (optional)

1. Combine oil, vinegar and brown sugar in small bowl; whisk until sugar dissolves. Toss with cucumbers. Marinate, covered, in refrigerator up to 4 hours.

2. Toss cucumbers and marinade with lettuce, noodles and peanuts, if desired, in large serving bowl.

CHINESE CRAB & CUCUMBER SALAD

Makes 4 servings

1 large cucumber, peeled

12 ounces crabmeat (fresh, pasteurized or thawed frozen), flaked

½ red bell pepper, diced

½ cup mayonnaise

3 tablespoons soy sauce

1 tablespoon dark sesame oil

1 teaspoon ground ginger

½ pound bean sprouts

1 tablespoon sesame seeds, toasted*

Fresh chives, cut into 1-inch pieces

*To toast sesame seeds, spread seeds in small skillet. Shake skillet over medium-low heat about 3 minutes or until seeds begin to pop and turn golden.

1. Cut cucumber in half lengthwise; scoop out seeds. Cut crosswise into ½-inch slices.

2. Combine cucumber, crabmeat and bell pepper in large bowl. Whisk mayonnaise, soy sauce, oil and ginger in small bowl until blended. Add to crabmeat mixture; toss gently to coat. Refrigerate 1 hour to allow flavors to blend.

3. To serve, arrange bean sprouts on individual serving plates. Spoon crabmeat mixture over sprouts; sprinkle with sesame seeds and chives.

BRAISED ASIAN CABBAGE

Makes 6 servings

½ small head green cabbage (about ½ pound)

1 small head bok choy (about ¾ pound)

½ cup fat-free reduced-sodium chicken broth

2 tablespoons rice wine vinegar

2 tablespoons reduced-sodium soy sauce

1 tablespoon packed brown sugar

¼ teaspoon red pepper flakes (optional)

1 tablespoon water

1 tablespoon cornstarch

1. Cut cabbage into 1-inch pieces. Trim and discard bottoms from bok choy; slice stems into ½-inch pieces. Cut tops of leaves into ½-inch slices; set aside.

2. Combine cabbage and bok choy stems in large nonstick skillet. Add broth, vinegar, soy sauce, brown sugar and red pepper flakes, if desired.

3. Bring to a boil over high heat. Reduce heat to medium. Cover and simmer 5 minutes or until vegetables are crisp-tender.

4. Stir water into cornstarch in small bowl until smooth. Stir into skillet. Cook and stir 1 minute or until sauce boils and thickens.

5. Stir in reserved bok choy leaves; cook 1 minute.

ASIAN FISH STEW

Makes 4 to 6 servings

8 to 10 dried black Chinese mushrooms

¼ cup reduced-sodium soy sauce

2 tablespoons Chinese rice wine

1 teaspoon chopped fresh ginger

Black pepper

½ pound medium shrimp, peeled and deveined

½ pound halibut, cubed

1 tablespoon vegetable oil

2 cloves garlic, chopped

2 cups diagonally sliced bok choy

1½ cups diagonally sliced napa cabbage

1 cup broccoli florets

2 cubes vegetable bouillon, dissolved in 2 cups hot water

½ cup bottled clam juice or water

2 tablespoons cold water

2 tablespoons cornstarch

¼ pound snow peas, stems removed

2 green onions with tops, sliced

Hot cooked rice (optional)

1. Place mushrooms in medium bowl; cover with warm water. Soak 20 to 40 minutes or until soft. Cut off and discard stems; cut caps into thin slices. Set aside.

2. Whisk soy sauce, rice wine, ginger and pepper in small bowl until well blended. Add shrimp and halibut; marinate at room temperature 10 minutes.

3. Meanwhile, heat oil in Dutch oven or large saucepan over medium-high heat. Add garlic; cook and stir 3 to 5 minutes or until softened. Stir in bok choy, cabbage and broccoli.

4. Drain seafood, reserving marinade. Pour prepared vegetable broth, clam juice and reserved marinade into Dutch oven; bring to a boil over high heat. Reduce heat to low. Simmer 5 to 10 minutes until vegetables are crisp-tender. Add seafood and mushrooms. Simmer 3 to 5 minutes or until shrimp are opaque and fish flakes easily when tested with fork.

5. Stir cold water and cornstarch in small bowl until smooth and well blended; stir into Dutch oven. Cook and stir until stew boils and is slightly thickened. Remove from heat; stir in snow peas and green onions. Serve over rice, if desired.

EGG DROP SOUP

Makes 2 servings

2 cans (about 14 ounces each) fat-free reduced-sodium chicken broth

1 tablespoon reduced-sodium soy sauce

2 teaspoons cornstarch

½ cup cholesterol-free egg substitute

¼ cup thinly sliced green onions

1. Bring broth to a boil in large saucepan over high heat. Reduce heat to medium-low.

2. Stir soy sauce and cornstarch in small bowl until smooth and well blended; stir into broth. Cook and stir 2 minutes or until slightly thickened.

3. Stirring constantly in one direction, slowly pour egg substitute in thin stream into soup.

4. Ladle soup into bowls; sprinkle with green onions.

MANDARIN CHICKEN SALAD

Makes 4 servings

3½ ounces thin rice noodles (rice vermicelli)

1 can (6 ounces) mandarin orange segments, chilled

⅓ cup honey

2 tablespoons rice wine vinegar

2 tablespoons reduced-sodium soy sauce

1 can (8 ounces) sliced water chestnuts, drained

4 cups shredded napa cabbage

1 cup shredded red cabbage

½ cup sliced radishes

4 thin slices red onion, cut in half and separated

3 boneless skinless chicken breasts (about 12 ounces), cooked and cut into strips

1. Place rice noodles in large bowl. Cover with hot water; soak 20 minutes or until soft. Drain.

2. Drain mandarin orange segments, reserving ⅓ cup liquid. Whisk reserved liquid, honey, vinegar and soy sauce in medium bowl. Add water chestnuts.

3. Divide noodles, cabbages, radishes and onion evenly among four serving plates. Top with chicken and orange segments. Remove water chestnuts from dressing and arrange on salads. Serve with remaining dressing.

SHRIMP and PASTA SALAD

Makes 4 servings

⅓ cup reduced-fat sour cream

¼ cup reduced-fat mayonnaise

1 tablespoon seasoned rice vinegar

1 teaspoon minced fresh garlic

¾ teaspoon minced fresh ginger

¼ teaspoon salt

¼ teaspoon white pepper

3 cups water

¼ pound fresh snow peas, trimmed

1 pound medium shrimp, peeled, deveined and cooked

2 cups mostaccioli, cooked and drained

½ cup red bell pepper strips

⅓ cup sliced green onions

6 cherry tomatoes, halved

Salad greens (endive, leaf lettuce, etc.)

1. Combine sour cream, mayonnaise, vinegar, garlic, ginger, salt and white pepper in small bowl. Mix well and set aside.

2. Bring water to a boil in medium saucepan. Add snow peas. Cook 2 minutes or until slightly softened and bright green. Drain and rinse with cold water. Place in large bowl. Add shrimp, mostaccioli, bell pepper and green onions. Pour sour cream mixture over shrimp mixture. Toss well to blend. Cover and refrigerate 1 hour. Add tomatoes and toss gently.

3. Arrange salad greens on plates; spoon shrimp salad over greens. Serve immediately.

BEEF & PORK

CHINESE PORK TENDERLOIN

Makes 8 servings

- 2 pork tenderloins (about 2 pounds total)
- 1 green bell pepper, cut into ½-inch dice
- 1 red bell pepper, cut into ½-inch dice
- 1 onion, thinly sliced
- 2 carrots, thinly sliced
- 1 jar (15 ounces) sweet and sour sauce
- 1 tablespoon soy sauce
- ½ teaspoon hot pepper sauce
- Hot cooked rice
- Sprigs fresh parsley or cilantro (optional)

Slow Cooker Directions

1. Cut pork into 1-inch cubes and place in 5- or 6-quart slow cooker.

2. Add bell peppers, onion, carrots, sweet and sour sauce, soy sauce and hot pepper sauce; stir to combine.

3. Cover; cook on LOW 6 to 7 hours or on HIGH 4 to 5 hours. Stir just before serving. Serve over rice and sprinkle with parsley, if desired.

SPICY CHINESE PEPPER STEAK

Makes 4 servings

1 boneless beef top sirloin
   steak (about 1 pound) or
   tenderloin tips, cut into
   thin strips

1 tablespoon cornstarch

3 cloves garlic, minced

½ teaspoon red pepper flakes

2 tablespoons peanut or
   canola oil, divided

1 green bell pepper, cut into
   thin strips

1 red bell pepper, cut into thin
   strips

¼ cup oyster sauce

2 tablespoons soy sauce

3 tablespoons chopped fresh
   cilantro or green onions

1. Combine beef, cornstarch, garlic and red pepper flakes in medium bowl; toss to coat.

2. Heat 1 tablespoon oil in wok or large skillet over medium-high heat. Add bell peppers; stir-fry 3 minutes. Remove to small bowl. Add remaining 1 tablespoon oil and beef mixture to wok; stir-fry 4 to 5 minutes or until beef is barely pink in center.

3. Add oyster sauce and soy sauce to wok; cook and stir 1 minute. Return bell peppers to wok; cook and stir 1 to 2 minutes or until sauce thickens. Sprinkle with cilantro.

SZECHUAN BEEF LO MEIN

Makes 4 servings

1 **boneless beef top sirloin steak (about 1 pound)**

4 **cloves garlic, minced**

2 **teaspoons minced fresh ginger**

¾ **teaspoon red pepper flakes, divided**

1 **tablespoon vegetable oil**

1 **can (about 14 ounces) vegetable broth**

1 **cup water**

2 **tablespoons reduced-sodium soy sauce**

1 **package (8 ounces) frozen mixed vegetables for stir-fry**

1 **package (9 ounces) refrigerated angel hair pasta**

¼ **cup chopped fresh cilantro (optional)**

1. Cut beef in half lengthwise, then crosswise into thin slices. Toss beef with garlic, ginger and ½ teaspoon red pepper flakes in medium bowl.

2. Heat oil in large nonstick skillet over medium-high heat. Add half of beef to skillet; stir-fry 2 minutes or until meat is barely pink in center. Remove from skillet; set aside. Repeat with remaining beef.

3. Add broth, water, soy sauce and remaining ¼ teaspoon red pepper flakes to skillet; bring to a boil over high heat. Add vegetables; return to a boil. Reduce heat to low; simmer, covered, 3 minutes or until vegetables are crisp-tender.

4. Uncover; stir in pasta. Return to a boil over high heat. Reduce heat to medium; simmer, uncovered, 2 minutes, separating pasta with two forks. Return beef and any accumulated juices to skillet; simmer 1 minute or until pasta is tender and beef is heated through. Sprinkle with cilantro, if desired.

SESAME CHILI BEEF

Makes 4 servings

1 beef flank steak (about
   1 pound)

3 tablespoons vegetable oil,
   divided

3 tablespoons reduced-
   sodium soy sauce

1 tablespoon rice wine or dry
   sherry

1 tablespoon cornstarch

2 teaspoons packed brown
   sugar

1 cup red, yellow and green
   bell peppers, cut into
   ¼-inch strips

1 cup broccoli florets

1 small piece fresh ginger
   (1 inch long), minced

2 cloves garlic, minced

1 hot chile pepper,* seeded
   and diced

1 teaspoon hot chili oil

   Sesame seeds (optional)

   Hot cooked rice (optional

*Chile peppers can sting and
irritate the skin, so wear rubber
gloves when handling peppers and
do not touch your eyes.

1. Cut flank steak in half lengthwise, then crosswise against the grain into ¼-inch-thick slices. Combine 1 tablespoon vegetable oil, soy sauce, wine, cornstarch and brown sugar in medium bowl. Add beef and toss to coat; set aside.

2. Heat wok over high heat 1 minute or until hot. Drizzle 1 tablespoon vegetable oil into wok and heat 30 seconds. Add half of beef mixture; stir-fry until well browned. Remove from wok; set aside. Repeat with remaining 1 tablespoon vegetable oil and beef mixture. Reduce heat to medium.

3. Add bell peppers, broccoli, ginger and garlic to wok; stir-fry 1 minute. Add chile pepper; stir-fry 1 minute.

4. Return beef and any accumulated juices to wok; add chili oil. Cook and stir until heated through. Sprinkle with sesame seeds and serve with rice, if desired.

BEEF and VEGETABLE STIR-FRY over RICE

Makes 4 servings

1 cup uncooked short or medium grain white rice

3 teaspoons peanut or vegetable oil, divided

3 eggs, beaten

2 cups broccoli florets

1 small yellow onion, cut into thin wedges

1 pound boneless beef top sirloin steak, cut crosswise into thin strips

2 teaspoons cornstarch

¼ cup beef or chicken broth

3 tablespoons tamari or soy sauce

2 teaspoons dark sesame oil

¼ teaspoon red pepper flakes

¼ cup chopped fresh cilantro

¼ cup chopped green onions

1. Cook rice according to package directions. Meanwhile, heat 1 teaspoon peanut oil in medium skillet over medium heat. Add eggs; cook 2 minutes or until bottom of omelet is set. Turn omelet over and cook 1 minute. Slide onto cutting board; let cool. Roll up omelet and cut crosswise into thin slices.

2. Heat 1 teaspoon peanut oil in same skillet; add broccoli and onion. Cook 4 to 5 minutes, stirring occasionally; transfer to bowl. Combine beef strips and cornstarch in medium bowl. Heat remaining 1 teaspoon peanut oil in same skillet; stir-fry beef 2 minutes. Add broth, tamari, sesame oil and red pepper flakes. Simmer 2 minutes or until sauce thickens.

3. Stir in sliced omelet, reserved vegetables, cilantro and green onions. Stir-fry 1 minute or until heated through. Spoon rice into four shallow bowls; top with beef mixture.

APRICOT BEEF
with SESAME NOODLES

Makes 4 to 6 servings

1 **beef top sirloin steak (about 1 pound)**

3 **tablespoons Dijon mustard**

3 **tablespoons soy sauce**

2 **packages (3 ounces each) uncooked ramen noodles, any flavor***

2 **tablespoons vegetable oil**

2 **cups (6 ounces) snow peas**

1 **medium red bell pepper, diced**

¾ **cup apricot preserves**

½ **cup beef broth**

3 **tablespoons chopped green onions**

2 **tablespoons toasted sesame seeds,** divided

*Discard seasoning packets.

**To toast sesame seeds, spread seeds in small skillet. Shake skillet over medium-low heat about 3 minutes or until seeds begin to pop and turn golden.

1. Cut beef lengthwise in half, then crosswise into ¼-inch strips. Combine beef, mustard and soy sauce in medium resealable food storage bag. Seal bag. Shake to evenly distribute marinade; refrigerate 4 hours or overnight.

2. Cook noodles according to package directions. Drain.

3. Heat oil in large skillet over medium-high heat until hot. Add half of beef with marinade; stir-fry 2 minutes. Remove to bowl. Repeat with remaining beef and marinade. Return beef to skillet. Add snow peas and bell pepper; stir-fry 2 minutes. Add noodles, preserves, broth, green onions and 1 tablespoon sesame seeds. Cook 1 minute or until heated through. Top with remaining 1 tablespoon sesame seeds before serving.

FUKIEN RED-COOKED PORK

Makes 4 to 5 servings

5¼ cups plus 3 tablespoons
water, divided

2 pounds boneless pork
shoulder, well trimmed,
cut into 1½-inch pieces

⅓ cup rice wine or dry sherry

⅓ cup soy sauce

¼ cup packed brown sugar

1 piece fresh ginger (about
1½ inches), peeled and
cut into strips

3 cloves garlic, chopped

1 teaspoon anise seeds

2 tablespoons cornstarch

1 pound carrots, diagonally
sliced

½ head napa cabbage
(about 1 pound), cored
and cut into 1-inch slices

1 teaspoon dark sesame oil

1. Pour 4 cups water into wok; bring to a boil over high heat. Add pork; return to a boil. Boil 2 minutes; drain and return pork to wok. Add 1¼ cups water, rice wine, soy sauce, brown sugar, ginger, garlic and anise; cover and bring to a boil. Reduce heat to low; cover and cook 1¼ hours or until pork is almost tender, stirring occasionally.

2. Stir remaining 3 tablespoons water into cornstarch in small bowl until smooth.

3. Add carrots to wok; cover and cook 20 minutes or until pork and carrots are fork-tender. Transfer to serving bowl with slotted spoon.

4. Add cabbage to liquid in wok; cover and cook over medium-high heat about 2 minutes or until wilted. Stir cornstarch mixture; add to wok. Cook until sauce boils and thickens. Return pork and carrots to wok; stir in oil until well blended.

Note: "Red cooking" is a Chinese cooking method in which meat or poultry is braised in soy sauce, giving the meat a deep, rich color.

CELLOPHANE NOODLES with MINCED PORK

Makes 4 servings

1 package (about 4 ounces) cellophane noodles

32 dried shiitake mushrooms

2 tablespoons minced fresh ginger

2 tablespoons black bean sauce

1½ cups chicken broth

1 tablespoon dry sherry

1 tablespoon soy sauce

2 tablespoons vegetable oil

6 ounces lean ground pork

3 green onions, sliced

1 jalapeño or other hot pepper,* seeded and finely chopped

Fresh cilantro sprigs and hot red peppers (optional)

*Jalapeño peppers can sting and irritate the skin, so wear rubber gloves when handling peppers and do not touch your eyes.

1. Place cellophane noodles and dried mushrooms in separate bowls; cover each with hot water. Let stand 30 minutes; drain.

2. Cut cellophane noodles into 4-inch pieces. Squeeze out excess water from mushrooms. Cut off and discard mushroom stems; cut caps into thin slices.

3. Combine ginger and black bean sauce in small bowl. Combine broth, sherry and soy sauce in medium bowl.

4. Heat oil in wok or large skillet over high heat. Add pork; stir-fry 2 minutes or until no longer pink. Add green onions, jalapeño pepper and black bean sauce mixture; stir-fry 1 minute.

5. Add broth mixture, noodles and mushrooms. Simmer, uncovered, about 5 minutes or until most of liquid is absorbed. Garnish with cilantro and red peppers.

SZECHUAN PORK STIR-FRY over SPINACH

Makes 2 servings

2 teaspoons dark sesame oil, divided

¾ cup matchstick carrots

8 ounces pork tenderloin, cut into thin strips

3 cloves garlic, minced

2 teaspoons minced fresh ginger

¼ teaspoon red pepper flakes

1 tablespoon reduced-sodium soy sauce

1 tablespoon dry sherry

2 teaspoons cornstarch

8 ounces baby spinach

2 teaspoons sesame seeds, toasted*

*To toast sesame seeds, spread seeds in small skillet. Shake skillet over medium-low heat about 3 minutes or until seeds begin to pop and turn golden.

1. Heat 1 teaspoon oil in large nonstick skillet over medium-high heat. Add carrots; stir-fry 3 minutes. Add pork, garlic, ginger and red pepper flakes; stir-fry 3 minutes or until pork is barely pink in center.

2. Stir soy sauce and sherry into cornstarch in small bowl until smooth. Add to skillet; cook 1 minute or until sauce is thickened.

3. Heat remaining 1 teaspoon oil in medium saucepan over medium-high heat. Add spinach; cover and cook 1 minute or until spinach is barely wilted.

4. Arrange spinach on two serving plates. Top with pork mixture; sprinkle with sesame seeds.

ASIAN BEEF with VEGETABLES

Makes 4 servings

1 pound ground beef or ground turkey

1 large onion, coarsely chopped

2 cloves garlic, minced

2½ cups (8 ounces) frozen mixed vegetable medley, such as carrots, broccoli and red peppers, thawed

½ cup stir-fry sauce

1 can (3 ounces) chow mein noodles

1. Cook beef and onion in wok or large skillet over medium-high heat until beef is no longer pink, stirring to break up meat. Drain fat.

2. Add garlic; stir-fry 1 minute. Add vegetables; stir-fry 2 minutes or until heated through.

3. Add stir-fry sauce; stir-fry 30 seconds or until hot. Serve over chow mein noodles.

BEEF and BROCCOLI

Makes 4 servings

1 pound beef tenderloin steaks

2 teaspoons minced fresh ginger

2 cloves garlic, minced

½ teaspoon vegetable oil

3 cups broccoli florets

¼ cup water

2 tablespoons teriyaki sauce

2 cups hot cooked rice

1. Cut beef crosswise into ⅛-inch-thick slices. Toss beef with ginger and garlic in medium bowl.

2. Heat oil in wok or large nonstick skillet over medium heat. Add half of beef mixture; stir-fry 2 to 3 minutes or until beef is barely pink in center. Remove to medium bowl. Repeat with remaining beef.

3. Add broccoli and water to wok; cover and steam 3 to 5 minutes or until broccoli is crisp-tender.

4. Return beef and any accumulated juices to wok. Add teriyaki sauce; cook and stir until heated through. Serve over rice.

SWEET GINGERED SPARERIBS

Makes 4 to 6 servings

½ **cup reduced-sodium soy sauce**

⅓ **cup honey**

¼ **cup dry sherry**

1 **clove garlic, minced**

¼ **to ½ teaspoon ground ginger**

4 **pounds pork spareribs, cut into 1- or 2-rib pieces**

1. Preheat oven to 350°F. Combine soy sauce, honey, sherry, garlic and ginger in small bowl; mix well. Line rimmed baking sheet with foil.

2. Arrange ribs on prepared baking sheet, meat side down. Brush soy sauce mixture generously over ribs; refrigerate remaining sauce. Cover ribs loosely with foil.

3. Bake 1 hour. Remove foil; turn ribs over and brush generously with soy sauce mixture. Bake, uncovered, 30 minutes or until ribs are tender, brushing occasionally with remaining soy sauce mixture.

CANTONESE TOMATO BEEF

Makes 4 servings

- 1 beef flank steak (about 1 pound)
- 2 tablespoons soy sauce
- 2 tablespoons dark sesame oil, divided
- 1 tablespoon plus 1 teaspoon cornstarch, divided
- 1 pound Chinese-style thin wheat noodles
- 1 cup beef broth
- 2 tablespoons packed brown sugar
- 1 tablespoon cider vinegar
- 2 tablespoons vegetable oil, divided
- 1 tablespoon minced fresh ginger
- 3 small onions, cut into wedges
- 2 pounds ripe tomatoes (5 large), cored and cut into wedges
- 1 green onion, diagonally cut into thin slices

1. Cut flank steak lengthwise in half, then crosswise against the grain into ¼-inch-thick slices. Combine soy sauce, 1 tablespoon sesame oil and 1 teaspoon cornstarch in large bowl. Add beef slices; toss to coat. Set aside.

2. Cook noodles according to package directions. Drain; toss with remaining 1 tablespoon sesame oil. Keep warm. Combine broth, brown sugar, remaining 1 tablespoon cornstarch and vinegar in small bowl; set aside.

3. Heat wok over high heat 1 minute. Drizzle 1 tablespoon vegetable oil into wok and heat 30 seconds. Add beef and marinade; stir-fry 5 minutes or until lightly browned. Remove beef from wok; reduce heat to medium. Add ginger and stir-fry 30 seconds.

4. Add remaining 1 tablespoon vegetable oil to wok. Add onion wedges; stir-fry 2 minutes. Stir in half of tomato wedges. Stir broth mixture; add to wok. Cook and stir until liquid boils and thickens.

5. Return beef and any juices to wok. Add remaining tomato wedges; cook and stir until heated through. Serve over noodles. Sprinkle with green onions.

MONGOLIAN BEEF

Makes 4 servings

1¼ pounds beef flank steak

¼ cup cornstarch

3 tablespoons vegetable oil, divided

3 cloves garlic, minced

2 teaspoons grated fresh ginger

½ cup water

½ cup soy sauce

⅓ cup packed dark brown sugar

Pinch red pepper flakes

2 green onions, diagonally sliced into 1-inch pieces

Hot cooked rice (optional)

1. Cut flank steak in half lengthwise, then cut crosswise (against the grain) into ¼-inch slices. Combine beef and cornstarch in medium bowl; toss to coat.

2. Heat 1 tablespoon oil in large skillet or wok over high heat. Add half of beef in single layer (do not crowd); cook 1 to 2 minutes per side or until browned. Remove to clean bowl. Repeat with remaining beef and 1 tablespoon oil.

3. Heat remaining 1 tablespoon oil in same skillet over medium heat. Add garlic and ginger; cook and stir 30 seconds. Add water, soy sauce, brown sugar and red pepper flakes; bring to a boil, stirring until well blended. Cook about 8 minutes or until slightly thickened.

4. Return beef to skillet; cook 2 to 3 minutes or until sauce thickens and beef is heated through. Stir in green onions. Serve over rice, if desired.

CHICKEN & TURKEY

SESAME HOISIN BEER-CAN CHICKEN

Makes 8 to 10 servings

1 can (12 ounces) beer,
   divided

½ cup hoisin sauce

2 tablespoons honey

1 tablespoon soy sauce

1 teaspoon chili garlic sauce

½ teaspoon dark sesame oil

1 whole chicken (3½ to
   4 pounds)

1. Prepare grill for indirect cooking over medium heat. Combine 2 tablespoons beer, hoisin sauce, honey, soy sauce, chili garlic sauce and oil in small bowl. Gently loosen skin of chicken over breast meat, legs and thighs. Spoon half of hoisin mixture evenly under skin and into cavity. Pour off beer until can is two-thirds full. Hold chicken upright with opening of cavity pointing down. Insert beer can into cavity.

2. Oil grill grid. Stand chicken upright on can over drip pan. Spread legs slightly to help support chicken. Cover; grill 30 minutes. Brush chicken with remaining hoisin mixture. Cover; grill 45 to 60 minutes or until chicken is cooked through (165°F). Use metal tongs to remove chicken and can to cutting board; let rest, standing up, 5 minutes. Carefully remove can and discard. Carve chicken and serve.

ALMOND CHICKEN

Makes 4 to 6 servings

1½ cups water

4 tablespoons dry sherry, divided

4½ teaspoons plus 1 tablespoon cornstarch, divided

4 teaspoons soy sauce

1 teaspoon chicken bouillon granules

1 egg white, beaten

½ teaspoon salt

4 whole boneless skinless chicken breasts, cut into 1-inch pieces

Vegetable oil for frying

½ cup blanched whole almonds (about 3 ounces)

1 large carrot, diced

1 teaspoon minced fresh ginger

6 green onions, cut into 1-inch pieces

3 stalks celery, diagonally cut into ½-inch pieces

8 mushrooms, sliced

½ cup sliced bamboo shoots (½ of 8-ounce can), drained

1. Combine water, 2 tablespoons sherry, 4½ teaspoons cornstarch, soy sauce and bouillon granules in small saucepan. Cook and stir over medium heat about 5 minutes or until mixture boils and thickens. Keep warm.

2. Combine remaining 2 tablespoons sherry, 1 tablespoon cornstarch, egg white and salt in medium bowl. Add chicken pieces; stir to coat well.

3. Heat oil in wok or large skillet over high heat to 375°F. Add half of chicken; cook 3 to 5 minutes or until light brown. Drain on paper towels. Repeat with remaining chicken.

4. Remove all but 2 tablespoons oil from wok. Add almonds; cook about 2 minutes or until golden. Transfer almonds to small bowl; set aside. Add carrot and ginger to wok; stir-fry 1 minute. Add green onions, celery, mushrooms and bamboo shoots; stir-fry about 3 minutes or until crisp-tender. Stir in chicken, almonds and sauce; cook and stir until heated through.

CHINESE TAKE-OUT STYLE CHICKEN and BROCCOLI

Makes 4 servings

4 cloves garlic, minced, divided

1 tablespoon fresh grated ginger

1/8 teaspoon red pepper flakes

12 ounces boneless skinless chicken breasts, cut into 2-inch pieces

1 ounce unsalted peanuts or slivered almonds

2 teaspoons canola oil, divided

1 medium onion, cut into 1/2-inch wedges

1 medium carrot, thinly sliced

2 cups broccoli florets, cut into 1-inch pieces

1 1/4 cups reduced-sodium chicken broth, divided

1 tablespoon cornstarch

1/8 teaspoon salt

2 tablespoons light soy sauce

1. To prepare marinade, combine half of garlic, ginger and red pepper flakes in small bowl. Place chicken in bowl; sprinkle garlic mixture on both sides. Cover; refrigerate 30 minutes, turning occasionally.

2. Heat large nonstick skillet over medium-high heat. Add peanuts; cook and stir 2 minutes or until lightly browned, stirring frequently. Remove from skillet; set aside.

3. Remove chicken from marinade; discard marinade. Add 1 teaspoon oil to skillet, tilting to coat lightly. Add chicken; cook and stir 2 minutes. Set aside on separate plate.

4. Add remaining 1 teaspoon oil to skillet; cook and stir onion and carrot 2 minutes. Add broccoli and 1/4 cup broth; bring to a boil over medium-high heat. Cover and cook 2 minutes or until broccoli is crisp-tender.

5. Meanwhile, combine remaining 1 cup broth with cornstarch in small bowl; whisk until cornstarch is completely dissolved. Add cornstarch mixture, chicken, remaining garlic and salt to skillet. Cook 1 minute or until thickened. Remove from heat, sprinkle with soy sauce and peanuts.

CHINESE CHICKEN STEW

Makes 6 servings

- **1 package (1 ounce) dried black Chinese mushrooms**
- **1 pound boneless skinless chicken thighs**
- **1 teaspoon Chinese five-spice powder**
- **¼ to ½ teaspoon red pepper flakes**
- **1 tablespoon peanut or vegetable oil**
- **1 large onion, coarsely chopped**
- **2 cloves garlic, minced**
- **1 can (about 14 ounces) chicken broth, divided**
- **1 tablespoon cornstarch**
- **1 large red bell pepper, cut into ¾-inch pieces**
- **1 tablespoon soy sauce**
- **2 large green onions, cut into ½-inch pieces**
- **1 tablespoon dark sesame oil**
- **3 cups hot cooked white rice**
- **¼ cup coarsely chopped fresh cilantro (optional)**

1. Place mushrooms in small bowl; cover with warm water. Soak 20 minutes to soften. Drain; squeeze out excess water. Discard stems; slice caps. Cut chicken into 1-inch pieces. Toss chicken with five-spice powder in small bowl. Season as desired with red pepper flakes.

2. Heat peanut oil in wok or large skillet over medium-high heat. Add coated chicken, onion and garlic; stir-fry 2 minutes or until chicken is cooked through.

3. Stir ¼ cup broth into cornstarch in small bowl until smooth. Add remaining broth to wok. Stir bell pepper, mushrooms and soy sauce into stew. Reduce heat to medium. Cover and simmer 10 minutes.

4. Stir cornstarch mixture; add to wok. Cook and stir 2 minutes or until sauce boils and thickens. Stir in green onions and sesame oil. Scoop ½ cup rice into each bowl. Ladle stew into soup bowls. Sprinkle with cilantro, if desired.

TURKEY LETTUCE WRAPS

Makes 12 wraps (6 servings)

1 teaspoon dark sesame oil

1 pound extra-lean ground turkey

½ cup sliced green onions

2 tablespoons minced fresh ginger

1 can (8 ounces) water chestnuts, chopped

1 teaspoon reduced-sodium soy sauce

¼ cup chopped fresh cilantro

12 large lettuce leaves

Chopped fresh mint and/ or chopped peanuts (optional)

1. Heat oil in large skillet over medium-high heat. Add turkey, green onions and ginger; cook 6 to 8 minutes, stirring to break up meat.

2. Add water chestnuts and soy sauce to skillet; cook 3 minutes or until turkey is no longer pink. Remove from heat; stir in cilantro.

3. Spoon ¼ cup turkey mixture onto each lettuce leaf. Top with chopped mint and/or peanuts, if desired. Roll up to enclose filling.

SWEET and SOUR CHICKEN

Makes 4 servings

2 tablespoons unseasoned rice vinegar

2 tablespoons reduced-sodium soy sauce

3 cloves garlic, minced

½ teaspoon minced fresh ginger

¼ teaspoon red pepper flakes (optional)

6 ounces boneless skinless chicken breasts, cut into ½-inch strips

1 teaspoon vegetable oil

3 green onions, cut into 1-inch pieces

1 large green bell pepper, cut into 1-inch pieces

1 tablespoon cornstarch

½ cup fat-free reduced-sodium chicken broth

2 tablespoons apricot fruit spread

1 can (11 ounces) mandarin orange segments, drained

2 cups hot cooked rice

1. Whisk vinegar, soy sauce, garlic, ginger and red pepper flakes, if desired, in medium bowl until smooth and well blended. Add chicken; toss to coat. Marinate 20 minutes at room temperature.

2. Heat oil in wok or large nonstick skillet over medium heat. Drain chicken; reserve marinade. Add chicken to wok; stir-fry 3 minutes. Stir in green onions and bell pepper.

3. Stir cornstarch into reserved marinade until well blended. Stir broth, fruit spread and marinade mixture into wok. Bring to a boil; cook 2 minutes or until chicken is cooked through and sauce is thickened. Add oranges; cook until heated through. Serve over rice.

NOODLES with SIMMERED CHICKEN

Makes 2 servings

- **4** dried black Chinese mushrooms
- **2** teaspoons dry sherry
- **1** boneless skinless chicken breast half, thinly sliced
- **8** ounces Chinese-style thin egg noodles
- **2** cups chicken broth
- **1** tablespoon soy sauce
- **¼** cup sliced bamboo shoots
- **1** small bunch watercress or ½ bunch fresh spinach leaves, cut into 2-inch wide stripes
- **1** teaspoon dark sesame oil
  Dash white pepper
- **2** green onions, thinly sliced

1. Place mushrooms in medium bowl; cover with warm water. Soak 20 to 40 minutes or until soft. Cut off and discard stems; cut caps into thin slices.

2. Meanwhile, sprinkle sherry over chicken slices in medium bowl; let stand 15 minutes. Cook noodles according to package directions until tender but still firm. Drain and rinse under cool water.

3. Combine broth and soy sauce in large saucepan; bring to a boil over high heat. Stir in mushrooms, chicken and bamboo shoots. Reduce heat to medium-low; cook about 4 minutes. Add watercress, sesame oil and pepper; cook 1 minute. Add noodles; cook until heated through. Ladle soup into bowls; sprinkle with green onions.

NOTE: To store leftover bamboo shoots, place shoots in jar with tight-fitting lid. Add water to cover and seal jar tightly. Bamboo shoots will keep, refrigerated, for up to 10 days, changing water daily.

ASIAN CHICKEN WINGS

Makes 32 appetizers

32 chicken wings, tips removed and split at joints

1 cup chopped red onion

1 cup soy sauce

¾ cup packed light brown sugar

¼ cup dry sherry

2 tablespoons chopped fresh ginger

2 cloves garlic, minced

Chopped fresh chives (optional)

Slow Cooker Directions

1. Preheat broiler. Broil wings about 5 minutes per side; transfer to slow cooker.

2. Combine red onion, soy sauce, brown sugar, sherry, ginger and garlic in large bowl. Add to slow cooker; stir to blend well. Cover; cook on LOW 5 to 6 hours or on HIGH 2 to 3 hours. Sprinkle with chives.

MU SHU TURKEY

Makes 6 servings

1 can (16 ounces) plums, drained and pitted

½ cup orange juice

¼ cup finely chopped onion

1 tablespoon minced fresh ginger

¼ teaspoon ground cinnamon

1 pound boneless turkey breast, cut into thin strips

6 (7-inch) flour tortillas

3 cups coleslaw mix

Slow Cooker Directions

1. Place plums in blender or food processor. Cover; process until almost smooth. Combine plums, orange juice, onion, ginger and cinnamon in slow cooker; mix well.

2. Place turkey over plum mixture. Cover; cook on LOW 3 to 4 hours.

3. Remove turkey from slow cooker. Divide evenly among tortillas. Spoon about 2 tablespoons plum sauce over turkey in each tortilla; top each with about ½ cup coleslaw mix. Fold bottom edge of tortilla over filling; fold in sides. Roll up to completely enclose filling. Use remaining plum sauce for dipping.

KUNG PAO CHICKEN

Makes 3 servings

5 teaspoons dry sherry, divided

5 teaspoons soy sauce, divided

3½ teaspoons cornstarch, divided

¼ teaspoon salt

3 boneless skinless chicken breasts (about 1 pound), cut into bite-size pieces

2 tablespoons chicken broth or water

1 tablespoon red wine vinegar

1½ teaspoons sugar

3 tablespoons vegetable oil, divided

⅓ cup salted peanuts

6 to 8 small dried red chiles

1½ teaspoons minced fresh ginger

2 green onions, cut into 1½-inch pieces

1. For marinade, combine 2 teaspoons sherry, 2 teaspoons soy sauce, 2 teaspoons cornstarch and salt in large bowl. Add chicken; stir to coat. Let stand 30 minutes.

2. Combine remaining 3 teaspoons sherry, 3 teaspoons soy sauce, 1½ teaspoons cornstarch, broth, vinegar and sugar in small bowl.

3. Heat 1 tablespoon oil in wok or large skillet over medium heat. Add peanuts; stir-fry until lightly toasted. Remove and set aside. Heat remaining 2 tablespoons oil in wok over medium heat. Add chiles; stir-fry about 1 minute or until chiles just begin to char.

4. Increase heat to high. Add chicken mixture; stir-fry 2 minutes. Add ginger; stir-fry about 1 minute or until chicken is cooked through. Stir in peanuts and green onions. Stir cornstarch mixture; add to wok. Cook and stir until sauce boils and thickens.

MOO GOO GAI PAN

Makes 4 servings

1 package (1 ounce) dried shiitake mushrooms

¼ cup reduced-sodium soy sauce

2 tablespoons rice vinegar

3 cloves garlic, minced

1 pound boneless skinless chicken breasts

½ cup chicken broth

1 tablespoon cornstarch

2 tablespoons peanut or vegetable oil, divided

1 can (about 7 ounces) straw mushrooms, rinsed and drained

3 green onions, cut into 1-inch pieces

Hot cooked Chinese egg noodles or rice (optional)

1. Place dried mushrooms in small bowl; cover with boiling water. Soak 20 minutes to soften. Drain; squeeze out excess water. Discard stems; slice caps.

2. Combine soy sauce, vinegar and garlic in medium bowl. Cut chicken crosswise into ½-inch strips. Add to soy sauce mixture; toss to coat. Marinate at room temperature 20 minutes. Stir broth into cornstarch in small bowl until smooth.

3. Heat 1 tablespoon oil in wok or large skillet over medium-high heat. Drain chicken, reserving marinade. Add chicken to wok; stir-fry 3 minutes or until cooked through. Remove to medium bowl. Heat remaining 1 tablespoon oil in wok. Add dried mushrooms, straw mushrooms and green onions; stir-fry 1 minute.

4. Stir cornstarch mixture; add to wok with reserved marinade. Bring to a boil; boil 1 minute or until sauce thickens. Return chicken and any accumulated juices to wok; cook until heated through. Serve over noodles, if desired.

SESAME CHICKEN

Makes 4 servings

1 pound boneless skinless chicken breasts or thighs, cut into 1-inch pieces

⅔ cup teriyaki sauce, divided

2 teaspoons cornstarch

1 tablespoon peanut or vegetable oil

2 cloves garlic, minced

2 green onions, cut into ½-inch slices

1 tablespoon sesame seeds, toasted*

1 teaspoon dark sesame oil

*To toast sesame seeds, spread seeds in small skillet. Shake skillet over medium-low heat 3 minutes or until seeds begin to pop and turn golden.

1. Combine chicken and ⅓ cup teriyaki sauce in medium bowl; toss to coat. Marinate in refrigerator 15 to 20 minutes.

2. Drain chicken; discard marinade. Stir remaining ⅓ cup teriyaki sauce into cornstarch in small bowl until smooth.

3. Heat peanut oil in wok or large skillet over medium-high heat. Add chicken and garlic; stir-fry 3 minutes or until chicken is cooked through. Stir cornstarch mixture; add to wok. Cook and stir 1 minute or until sauce boils and thickens. Stir in green onions, sesame seeds and sesame oil.

HOT CHINESE CHICKEN SALAD

Makes 6 servings

8 ounces fresh or steamed Chinese egg noodles

¼ cup fat-free reduced-sodium chicken broth

2 tablespoons reduced-sodium soy sauce

2 tablespoons rice wine vinegar

1 tablespoon rice wine or dry sherry

1 teaspoon sugar

½ teaspoon red pepper flakes

3 teaspoons vegetable oil, divided

1 clove garlic, minced

1½ cups fresh snow peas, diagonally sliced

1 cup thinly sliced red or green bell pepper

1 pound boneless skinless chicken breasts, cut into ½-inch pieces

1 cup thinly sliced red or green cabbage

2 green onions, thinly sliced

1. Cook noodles in boiling water 4 to 5 minutes or until tender. Drain; set aside. Blend broth, soy sauce, vinegar, rice wine, sugar and red pepper flakes in small bowl; set aside.

2. Heat 1 teaspoon oil in large nonstick skillet or wok. Add garlic, snow peas and bell pepper; cook 1 to 2 minutes or until vegetables are crisp-tender. Remove from skillet; set aside.

3. Heat remaining 2 teaspoons oil in skillet. Add chicken; cook 3 to 4 minutes or until chicken is no longer pink. Add cabbage, cooked vegetables and noodles. Stir in sauce; toss until well blended. Cook and stir 1 to 2 minutes or until heated through. Sprinkle with green onions before serving.

CHICKEN LETTUCE WRAPS

Makes 6 to 8 servings

1 tablespoon vegetable oil

1 small onion, finely chopped

5 ounces cremini mushrooms, finely chopped (about 2 cups)

1 pound ground chicken

¼ cup hoisin sauce

2 tablespoons soy sauce

1 tablespoon rice vinegar

1 tablespoon sriracha sauce

1 tablespoon oyster sauce

2 cloves garlic, minced

1 teaspoon grated fresh ginger

1 teaspoon dark sesame oil

½ cup finely chopped water chestnuts

2 green onions, thinly sliced

1 head butter lettuce

1. Heat vegetable oil in large skillet over medium-high heat. Add onion; cook and stir 2 minutes. Add mushrooms; cook about 8 minutes or until lightly browned and liquid has evaporated, stirring occasionally.

2. Add chicken; cook about 8 minutes or until no longer pink, stirring to break up meat. Stir in hoisin sauce, soy sauce, vinegar, sriracha sauce, oyster sauce, garlic, ginger and sesame oil; cook 4 minutes. Add water chestnuts; cook and stir 2 minutes or until heated through. Remove from heat; stir in green onions.

3. Separate lettuce leaves. Spoon about ¼ cup chicken mixture into each lettuce leaf. Serve immediately.

FISH & SEAFOOD

ASIAN BAKED COD

Makes 4 servings

2 tablespoons reduced-sodium soy sauce

2 tablespoons apple juice

1 tablespoon finely chopped fresh ginger

2 cloves garlic, minced

1 teaspoon crushed Szechuan peppercorns

4 cod fillets (about 1 pound)

4 green onions, thinly sliced

1. Preheat oven to 375°F. Spray roasting pan with nonstick cooking spray.

2. Whisk soy sauce, apple juice, ginger, garlic and peppercorns in small bowl until well blended. Place fish in prepared pan; pour soy sauce mixture over fish.

3. Bake 10 minutes or until fish is opaque and flakes easily when tested with fork.

4. Remove fish to serving dish; pour pan juices over fish. Sprinkle with green onions.

GRILLED SWORDFISH
with HOT RED SAUCE

Makes 4 servings

2 tablespoons Sesame Salt (recipe follows)

4 swordfish or halibut steaks (about 1½ pounds total)

¼ cup chopped green onions

2 tablespoons hot bean paste

2 tablespoons soy sauce

4 teaspoons sugar

4 cloves garlic, minced

1 tablespoon dark sesame oil

⅛ teaspoon black pepper

1. Prepare Sesame Salt.

2. Rinse swordfish and pat dry with paper towels. Place in shallow glass dish.

3. Combine green onions, 2 tablespoons Sesame Salt, hot bean paste, soy sauce, sugar, garlic, oil and pepper in small bowl; mix well.

4. Spread mixture over both sides of fish; cover with plastic wrap. Marinate in refrigerator 30 minutes.

5. Prepare grill for direct cooking or preheat broiler. Oil grid or spray broiler rack with nonstick cooking spray.

6. Remove fish from marinade; discard remaining marinade. Grill fish over medium-high heat or broil 4 to 5 minutes per side or until fish is opaque.

Sesame Salt: Heat small skillet over medium heat. Add ¼ cup sesame seeds; cook and stir about 3 minutes or until seeds are golden. Cool. Crush toasted sesame seeds and 1 teaspoon coarse salt with mortar and pestle or process in clean spice grinder. Store in airtight container in refrigerator.

CHINESE CRAB CAKES

Makes 4 servings

1 **pound fresh* or canned pasteurized lump crabmeat**

½ **cup plus ⅓ cup panko bread crumbs, divided**

2 **eggs**

2 **green onions, finely chopped**

1 **tablespoon dark sesame oil**

1 **tablespoon grated fresh ginger**

1 **tablespoon Chinese hot mustard**

2 **tablespoons peanut or canola oil, divided**

½ **cup prepared sweet and sour sauce**

*Choose special grade crabmeat for this recipe. It is less expensive and already flaked but just as flavorful as backfin, lump or claw meat. Look for it in the refrigerated seafood section of the supermarket. Shelf-stable canned crabmeat can be substituted.

1. Combine crabmeat, ½ cup panko, eggs, green onions, sesame oil, ginger and mustard in large bowl; mix well.

2. Shape level ⅓ cupfuls of mixture into eight patties about ½ inch thick. (At this point patties may be covered and refrigerated up to 2 hours.)

3. Heat 1 tablespoon peanut oil in large nonstick skillet over medium heat. Place remaining ⅓ cup panko in shallow dish; dip each crab cake lightly in panko to coat both sides.

4. Add four crab cakes to skillet; cook 3 to 4 minutes per side or until golden brown and heated through. (Crab cakes will be soft, so turn carefully.) Remove to plate; tent with foil to keep warm. Repeat with remaining 1 tablespoon peanut oil and four crab cakes. Serve with sweet and sour sauce.

ASIAN SALMON over GARLICKY SPINACH

Makes 4 servings

1½ tablespoons red miso

1 teaspoon minced ginger

¼ teaspoon red pepper flakes

1 tablespoon plus
  2 teaspoons water,
  divided

4 skinless salmon fillets
  (5 ounces each)

4 cloves garlic, minced

1 bag (10 ounces) fresh
  spinach leaves or baby
  spinach

1. Preheat broiler. Combine miso, ginger and red pepper flakes in medium bowl; stir in 2 teaspoons water until blended. Reserve ½ teaspoon mixture in small bowl; spread remaining mixture over tops of salmon fillets. Place salmon on broiler pan or baking sheet.

2. Broil 4 to 5 inches from heat source 5 to 6 minutes or until salmon is opaque in center.

3. Meanwhile, spray large skillet with nonstick cooking spray; heat over medium heat. Add garlic; cook and stir 2 minutes. Stir remaining 1 tablespoon water into reserved miso mixture; mix well. Stir into garlic in skillet. Add spinach to skillet; cook 1 to 2 minutes or just until wilted, turning with tongs constantly. Transfer to serving plates; top with salmon.

NOODLES with BABY SHRIMP

Makes 4 to 6 servings

1 package (3¾ ounces) bean thread noodles

1 tablespoon vegetable oil

3 green onions, cut into 1-inch pieces

1 package (16 ounces) frozen stir-fry vegetables

1 cup vegetable broth

8 ounces frozen cooked baby shrimp

1 tablespoon soy sauce

2 teaspoons dark sesame oil

¼ teaspoon black pepper

1. Place noodles in large bowl. Cover with warm water; let stand 10 to 15 minutes or just until softened. Drain noodles; cut into 5- to 6-inch pieces.

2. Heat wok or large skillet over high heat 1 minute. Add vegetable oil; heat 30 seconds. Add green onions; stir-fry 1 minute. Add vegetables; stir-fry 2 minutes. Stir in broth; bring to a boil. Reduce heat to low; cover and cook 5 minutes or until vegetables are crisp-tender.

3. Add shrimp; cook just until thawed. Stir in noodles, soy sauce, sesame oil and pepper; stir-fry until heated through.

GRILLED ASIAN SALMON

Makes 4 servings

- **3 tablespoons soy sauce**
- **2 tablespoons dry sherry**
- **2 cloves garlic, minced**
- **4 salmon fillet pieces or steaks (about 1 pound)**
- **2 tablespoons finely chopped fresh cilantro**

1. Combine soy sauce, sherry and garlic in shallow dish; mix well. Add salmon; turn to coat. Cover and marinate in refrigerator at least 30 minutes or up to 2 hours. Prepare grill for direct cooking.

2. Oil grid. Prepare grill for direct cooking. Remove salmon from dish, reserving marinade.

3. Grill or broil salmon, skin side down, 10 minutes or until center is opaque, basting with reserved marinade after 5 minutes of cooking. Discard any remaining marinade. Sprinkle with cilantro.

CHILLED SHRIMP
with CHINESE MUSTARD SAUCE

Makes 6 servings

1 cup water

½ cup dry white wine

2 tablespoons reduced-sodium soy sauce

½ teaspoon Szechuan pepper or whole black peppercorns

1 pound large raw shrimp, peeled and deveined (with tails on)

¼ cup prepared sweet and sour sauce

2 teaspoons hot Chinese mustard

1. Combine water, wine, soy sauce and pepper in medium saucepan; bring to a boil over high heat.

2. Add shrimp. Reduce heat to medium; cover and simmer 2 to 3 minutes or until shrimp are opaque. Drain well; cover and refrigerate until chilled.

3. For mustard sauce, combine sweet and sour sauce and mustard in small bowl; mix well. Serve with shrimp.

Substitution: If you are unable to find hot Chinese mustard or simply want a sauce with less heat, substitute a spicy brown or Dijon mustard.

Tip: For this quick and easy recipe, the shrimp can be prepared up to 1 day in advance.

EASY SEAFOOD STIR-FRY

Makes 4 servings

1 package (1 ounce) dried black Chinese mushrooms*

½ cup fat-free reduced-sodium chicken broth

2 tablespoons dry sherry

1 tablespoon reduced-sodium soy sauce

4½ teaspoons cornstarch

1 teaspoon vegetable oil, divided

8 ounces bay scallops or halved sea scallops

4 ounces medium raw shrimp, peeled and deveined

2 cloves garlic, minced

6 ounces (2 cups) fresh snow peas, cut diagonally into halves

2 cups hot cooked rice

¼ cup thinly sliced green onions

*Or substitute 1½ cups sliced mushrooms and omit step 1.

1. Place mushrooms in medium bowl; cover with warm water. Soak 20 to 40 minutes or until soft. Drain and squeeze out excess water. Discard stems; thinly slice caps.

2. Whisk broth, sherry, soy sauce and cornstarch in small bowl until smooth.

3. Heat ½ teaspoon oil in wok or large nonstick skillet over medium heat. Add scallops, shrimp and garlic; stir-fry 3 minutes or until seafood is opaque. Remove to large plate.

4. Heat remaining ½ teaspoon oil in wok. Add mushrooms and snow peas; stir-fry 3 minutes or until snow peas are crisp-tender. Stir broth mixture; add to wok. Stir-fry 2 minutes or until sauce boils and thickens.

5. Return seafood and any accumulated juices to wok; stir-fry until heated through. Serve with rice; sprinkle with green onions.

HOT and SOUR SHRIMP

Makes 4 servings

½ **(1-ounce) package dried shiitake or black Chinese mushrooms***

½ **small unpeeled cucumber**

1 **tablespoon packed brown sugar**

2 **teaspoons cornstarch**

3 **tablespoons rice vinegar**

2 **tablespoons reduced-sodium soy sauce**

1 **tablespoon vegetable oil**

1 **pound medium raw shrimp, peeled and deveined (with tails on)**

2 **cloves garlic, minced**

¼ **teaspoon red pepper flakes**

1 **large red bell pepper, cut into short, thin strips**

Hot cooked Chinese egg noodles or oriental flavored ramen noodles** (optional)

*Or substitute ¾ cup sliced mushrooms and omit step 1.

**Discard seasoning packet.

1. Place mushrooms in small bowl; cover with warm water. Soak 20 minutes to soften. Drain and squeeze out excess water. Discard stems; slice caps.

2. Cut cucumber in half lengthwise; scrape out seeds. Cut crosswise into ¼-inch slices.

3. Combine brown sugar and cornstarch in small bowl. Whisk in vinegar and soy sauce until smooth.

4. Heat oil in wok or large nonstick skillet over medium heat. Add shrimp, garlic and red pepper flakes; stir-fry 1 minute. Add mushrooms and bell pepper strips; stir-fry 2 minutes or until shrimp are pink and opaque.

5. Stir vinegar mixture; add to wok. Cook and stir 30 seconds or until sauce boils and thickens. Add cucumber; stir-fry until heated through. Serve over noodles, if desired.

BROILED HUNAN FISH FILLETS

Makes 4 servings

- **3** tablespoons reduced-sodium soy sauce
- **1** tablespoon finely chopped green onion
- **2** teaspoons dark sesame oil
- **1** clove garlic, minced
- **1** teaspoon minced fresh ginger
- **¼** teaspoon red pepper flakes
- **1** pound red snapper, scrod or cod fillets

1. Combine soy sauce, green onion, oil, garlic, ginger and red pepper flakes in small bowl.

2. Spray rack of broiler pan with nonstick cooking spray. Place fish on rack; brush with soy sauce mixture.

3. Broil 4 to 5 inches from heat 10 minutes or until fish begins to flake when tested with fork.

ORANGE ALMOND SCALLOPS

Makes 4 servings

- 3 tablespoons orange juice
- 1 tablespoon reduced-sodium soy sauce
- 1 clove garlic, minced
- 1 pound bay scallops or halved sea scallops
- 1 tablespoon cornstarch
- 1 teaspoon vegetable oil, divided
- 1 green bell pepper, cut into short, thin strips
- 1 can (8 ounces) sliced water chestnuts, drained and rinsed
- 3 tablespoons toasted blanched almonds
- 3 cups cooked white rice
- ½ teaspoon finely grated orange peel

1. Combine orange juice, soy sauce and garlic in medium bowl. Add scallops; toss to coat. Marinate at room temperature 15 minutes or cover and refrigerate up to 1 hour.

2. Drain scallops; reserve marinade. Stir marinade into cornstarch in small bowl until smooth.

3. Heat ½ teaspoon oil in wok or large nonstick skillet over medium heat. Add scallops; stir-fry 2 minutes or until scallops are opaque. Remove to plate.

4. Heat remaining ½ teaspoon oil in wok. Add bell pepper and water chestnuts; stir-fry 3 minutes.

5. Return scallops along with any accumulated juices to wok. Stir marinade mixture and add to wok. Stir-fry 1 minute or until sauce boils and thickens. Stir in almonds. Serve over rice; sprinkle with orange peel. Garnish, if desired.

BEIJING FILLET OF SOLE

Makes 4 servings

- **2 tablespoons reduced-sodium soy sauce**
- **2 teaspoons dark sesame oil**
- **4 sole fillets (about 6 ounces each)**
- **1¼ cups shredded cabbage or coleslaw mix**
- **½ cup crushed chow mein noodles**
- **1 egg white, lightly beaten**
- **2 teaspoons sesame seeds**

1. Preheat oven to 350°F. Line shallow baking pan with foil.

2. Whisk soy sauce and oil in small bowl until well blended. Place fish in shallow dish. Lightly brush both sides of fish with soy sauce mixture; reserve remaining soy sauce mixture.

3. Combine cabbage, noodles, egg white and remaining soy sauce mixture in medium bowl; toss gently to coat. Spoon evenly into center of each fillet and roll up. Place seam side down in prepared pan. Sprinkle with sesame seeds.

4. Bake 25 to 30 minutes or until fish begins to flake when tested with fork.

TOFU & VEGETARIAN

SPICY FRIED RICE with TOFU
Makes 4 servings

2 eggs

4½ teaspoons vegetable oil, divided

1 tablespoon minced garlic

1 tablespoon minced fresh ginger

½ teaspoon red pepper flakes

2 cups thinly sliced Chinese cabbage

1 cup chopped carrots

1 cup frozen green peas, thawed

3 cups cooked white rice

4 ounces firm tofu, drained and cut into ½-inch cubes

¼ cup vegetable broth

¼ cup soy sauce

3 tablespoons dry sherry

2 teaspoons balsamic vinegar

1. Lightly beat eggs in small bowl. Heat 1½ teaspoons oil in wok or large skillet over medium-high heat. Add eggs; cook and stir 2 to 3 minutes until set. Remove from wok; cut into small pieces. Set aside.

2. Heat remaining 3 teaspoons oil in same wok over high heat. Add garlic, ginger and red pepper flakes; cook 30 seconds or until fragrant. Add cabbage, carrots and peas; cook 5 to 10 minutes until carrots are crisp-tender.

3. Stir in rice, tofu, broth, soy sauce, sherry and vinegar; cook and stir 3 minutes. Remove from heat. Stir in eggs.

DRAGON TOFU

Makes 2 servings

1 package (14 ounces) firm
   tofu, drained

¼ cup soy sauce

1 tablespoon creamy peanut
   butter

1 medium zucchini

1 medium yellow squash

1 medium red bell pepper

2 teaspoons peanut or
   vegetable oil

½ teaspoon hot chili oil

2 cloves garlic, minced

2 cups packed torn fresh
   spinach

   Hot cooked rice

¼ cup coarsely chopped
   cashew nuts or peanuts

1. Press tofu lightly between paper towels; cut into ¾-inch triangles or squares. Place in single layer in shallow dish. Whisk soy sauce into peanut butter in small bowl until smooth. Pour mixture over tofu; stir gently to coat. Let stand at room temperature 20 minutes.

2. Meanwhile, cut zucchini and yellow squash lengthwise into ¼-inch-thick slices; cut each slice into 2-inch strips. Cut bell pepper into 2-inch strips.

3. Heat peanut oil and chili oil in large wok or skillet over medium-high heat. Add garlic, zucchini, yellow squash and bell pepper; stir-fry 3 minutes. Add tofu mixture; cook 2 minutes or until tofu is heated through and sauce is slightly thickened, stirring occasionally. Stir in spinach; remove from heat. Serve over rice. Sprinkle with cashews.

BEAN THREADS with TOFU and VEGETABLES

Makes 6 servings

- **8 ounces firm tofu, drained and cubed**
- **1 tablespoon dark sesame oil**
- **3 teaspoons reduced-sodium soy sauce, divided**
- **1 can (about 14 ounces) fat-free reduced-sodium vegetable broth**
- **1 package (3¾ ounces) uncooked bean thread noodles**
- **1 package (16 ounces) frozen mixed vegetable medley such as broccoli, carrots and water chestnuts, thawed**
- **¼ cup rice wine vinegar**
- **½ teaspoon red pepper flakes**

1. Place tofu on shallow plate; drizzle with oil and 1½ teaspoons soy sauce.

2. Combine broth and remaining 1½ teaspoons soy sauce in deep skillet or large saucepan. Bring to a boil over high heat; reduce heat. Add bean threads; simmer, uncovered, 7 minutes or until liquid is absorbed, stirring occasionally (to separate noodles).

3. Stir in vegetables and vinegar; heat through. Stir in tofu mixture and red pepper flakes; heat through.

BUDDHA'S DELIGHT

Makes 2 servings

- **1 package (1 ounce) dried black Chinese mushrooms**
- **1 package (14 ounces) firm tofu, drained**
- **1 tablespoon peanut or vegetable oil**
- **2 cups diagonally cut 1-inch asparagus pieces**
- **1 medium onion, cut into thin wedges**
- **2 cloves garlic, minced**
- **½ cup vegetable broth**
- **3 tablespoons hoisin sauce**
- **¼ cup coarsely chopped fresh cilantro or thinly sliced green onions**

1. Place mushrooms in medium bowl; cover with warm water. Soak 20 to 40 minutes or until soft. Drain mushrooms, reserving soaking liquid. Discard stems; thinly slice caps.

2. Meanwhile, place tofu on plate or cutting board lined with paper towels; cover with additional paper towels. Place flat, heavy object on top; let stand 15 minutes. Cut tofu into ¾-inch cubes or triangles.

3. Heat oil in wok or large skillet over medium-high heat. Add asparagus, onion and garlic; stir-fry 4 minutes.

4. Add mushrooms, ¼ cup reserved mushroom liquid, broth and hoisin sauce; cook over medium-low heat 2 to 3 minutes or until asparagus is crisp-tender.

5. Stir in tofu; cook until heated through. Sprinkle with cilantro.

MA PO TOFU

Makes 4 servings

1 package (14 ounces) firm tofu, drained and pressed*

2 tablespoons soy sauce

2 teaspoons minced fresh ginger

1 cup vegetable broth, divided

2 tablespoons black bean sauce

1 tablespoon Thai sweet chili sauce

1 tablespoon cornstarch

2 tablespoons vegetable oil

1 green bell pepper, cut into bite-size pieces

2 cloves garlic, minced

1½ cups broccoli florets

¼ cup chopped fresh cilantro (optional)

Hot cooked rice

*Cut tofu in half horizontally and place it between layers of paper towels. Place a weighted cutting board on top; let stand 15 to 30 minutes.

1. Cut tofu into cubes. Place in shallow dish; sprinkle with soy sauce and ginger.

2. Whisk ¼ cup broth, black bean sauce, chili sauce and cornstarch in small bowl until smooth and well blended; set aside.

3. Heat oil in wok or large skillet over high heat. Add bell pepper and garlic; stir-fry 2 minutes. Add remaining ¾ cup broth and broccoli; bring to a boil. Reduce heat; cover and simmer 3 minutes or until broccoli is crisp-tender.

4. Stir sauce mixture; add to wok. Stir-fry 1 minute or until sauce boils and thickens. Stir in tofu; simmer, uncovered, until heated through. Sprinkle with cilantro, if desired. Serve with rice.

TOFU ZUCCHINI STIR-FRY

Makes 4 servings

1¾ cups water

3 tablespoons packed brown sugar

3 tablespoons soy sauce

2 tablespoons lime juice

1 tablespoon anchovy paste or 2 tablespoons fish sauce

2 large zucchini

4 tablespoons vegetable oil, divided

1 package (14 ounces) firm tofu, pressed and cut into cubes or strips

2 eggs, lightly beaten

2 cloves garlic, minced

1 tablespoon paprika

¼ to ½ teaspoon ground red pepper

8 ounces fresh bean sprouts, divided

½ cup coarsely chopped unsalted dry-roasted peanuts

4 green onions with tops, cut into 1-inch lengths

½ lime, cut lengthwise into 4 wedges (optional)

1. Combine water, brown sugar, soy sauce, lime juice and anchovy paste in small bowl; set aside.

2. Spiral zucchini with fine spiral blade;* cut into desired lengths. Heat 1 tablespoon oil in wok over medium-high heat. Add zucchini; stir-fry 2 to 3 minutes or until crisp-tender. Transfer to large bowl.

3. Heat 1 tablespoon oil in wok over medium-high heat. Add tofu; cook about 5 minutes or until browned on all sides, turning occasionally. Transfer to bowl with zucchini.

4. Heat wok over medium heat about 30 seconds or until hot. Drizzle 1 tablespoon oil into wok and heat 15 seconds. Add eggs; cook 1 minute or just until set on bottom. Turn eggs over and stir to scramble until cooked but not dry. Transfer to bowl with zucchini.

5. Drizzle remaining 1 tablespoon oil into wok and heat 15 seconds. Add garlic, paprika and red pepper; cook 30 seconds or until fragrant. Add zucchini, tofu, egg and sauce mixture; stir-fry 3 to 5 minutes or until zucchini is tender and coated with sauce. Stir in bean sprouts, peanuts and green onions; cook about 1 minute or until onions begin to wilt. Serve immediately with lime wedges.

*If you don't have a spiralizer, purchase zucchini noodles or cut zucchini into thin strips.

SIDES, RICE & NOODLES

VEGETABLE LO MEIN

Makes 4 servings

8 ounces uncooked Chinese egg noodles or thin spaghetti

2 egg whites

1 egg

1 green onion, thinly sliced

1 tablespoon dark sesame oil

4 ounces shiitake mushrooms, tough stems discarded, caps sliced or 1 package (4 ounces) sliced exotic mushrooms

2 cups thinly sliced bok choy (leaves and stems)

1 small red or yellow bell pepper, cut into strips

½ cup reduced-sodium vegetable broth

¼ cup reduced-sodium teriyaki sauce

Chopped peanuts (optional)

Chopped fresh cilantro (optional)

1. Cook noodles according to package directions; drain.

2. Beat egg whites and egg in small bowl until foamy. Stir in green onion. Spray large nonstick skillet with nonstick cooking spray; heat over medium heat. Add egg mixture; cook, without stirring, 2 to 3 minutes or until bottom is set. Gently turn omelet; cook 1 minute or until bottom is set. Remove to cutting board.

3. Heat oil in same skillet over medium-high heat. Add mushrooms, bok choy and bell pepper; stir-fry 4 to 5 minutes or until vegetables are tender. Add broth and teriyaki sauce; cook and stir 2 minutes. Remove to large bowl. Add noodles; toss to coat.

4. Cut omelet into strips. Add to noodle mixture; stir gently to combine. Sprinkle with peanuts and cilantro, if desired.

ZUCCHINI SHANGHAI STYLE

Makes 4 servings

4 dried Chinese black mushrooms

½ cup fat-free reduced-sodium chicken broth

2 tablespoons ketchup

2 teaspoons dry sherry

1 teaspoon reduced-sodium soy sauce

1 teaspoon red wine vinegar

¼ teaspoon sugar

1½ teaspoons vegetable oil, divided

1 teaspoon minced fresh ginger

1 clove garlic, minced

1 large tomato, peeled, seeded and chopped

1 green onion, finely chopped

4 tablespoons water, divided

1 teaspoon cornstarch

1 pound zucchini (about 3 medium), diagonally cut into 1-inch pieces

½ small yellow onion, cut into wedges and separated

1. Soak mushrooms in warm water 20 minutes. Drain, reserving ¼ cup liquid. Squeeze out excess water. Discard stems; slice caps. Combine reserved ¼ cup mushroom liquid, broth, ketchup, sherry, soy sauce, vinegar and sugar in small bowl. Set aside.

2. Heat 1 teaspoon oil in large saucepan over medium heat. Add ginger and garlic; cook 10 seconds. Add mushrooms, tomato and green onion; cook 1 minute. Add broth mixture; bring to a boil over high heat. Reduce heat to medium; simmer 10 minutes.

3. Combine 1 tablespoon water and cornstarch in small bowl; set aside. Heat remaining ½ teaspoon oil in large nonstick skillet or wok over medium heat. Add zucchini and yellow onion; stir-fry 30 seconds. Add remaining 3 tablespoons water. Cover and cook 3 to 4 minutes or until vegetables are crisp-tender, stirring occasionally. Add tomato mixture to skillet. Stir cornstarch mixture and add to skillet. Cook until sauce boils and thickens.

MOO SHU VEGETABLES

Makes 8 servings

½ **(1-ounce) package dried black Chinese mushrooms (6 or 7 mushrooms)**

2 **tablespoons vegetable oil**

2 **cloves garlic, minced**

2 **cups shredded napa or green cabbage**

1 **red bell pepper, cut into short, thin strips**

1 **cup fresh or canned bean sprouts, rinsed and drained**

2 **green onions, cut into short, thin strips**

1 **tablespoon teriyaki sauce**

⅓ **cup plum sauce**

8 **(6-inch) flour tortillas, warmed**

1. Place mushrooms in medium bowl; cover with warm water. Soak 20 minutes to soften. Drain mushrooms; squeeze out excess water. Discard stems; thinly slice caps.

2. Heat oil in wok or large nonstick skillet over medium heat. Add garlic; stir-fry 30 seconds. Add cabbage, mushrooms and bell pepper; stir-fry 3 minutes. Add bean sprouts and green onions; stir-fry 2 minutes. Add teriyaki sauce; stir-fry 30 seconds or until heated through.

3. Spread about 2 teaspoons plum sauce on each tortilla. Spoon heaping ¼ cup vegetable mixture over sauce; roll up to enclose filling. Serve immediately.

SESAME NOODLE CAKE

Makes 4 servings

4 ounces vermicelli or Chinese egg noodles

1 tablespoon soy sauce

1 tablespoon peanut or vegetable oil

½ teaspoon dark sesame oil

1. Cook vermicelli according to package directions; drain well. Place in large bowl. Toss with soy sauce until sauce is absorbed.

2. Heat 10- or 11-inch nonstick skillet over medium heat. Add peanut oil; heat until hot. Add vermicelli mixture; pat into an even layer with spatula.

3. Cook, uncovered, 6 minutes or until bottom is lightly browned. Invert onto plate, then slide back into skillet, browned side up. Cook 4 minutes or until bottom is well browned. Drizzle with sesame oil. Transfer to serving platter and cut into quarters.

Serving Suggestion: Serve Sesame Noodle Cake with your choice of stir-fry.

SZECHUAN EGGPLANT

Makes 4 servings

- **1 pound Asian eggplants or regular eggplant, peeled**
- **2 tablespoons peanut or vegetable oil**
- **2 cloves garlic, minced**
- **¼ teaspoon red pepper flakes or ½ teaspoon hot chili oil**
- **¼ cup vegetable broth**
- **¼ cup hoisin sauce**
- **3 green onions, cut into 1-inch pieces**
- **Toasted sesame seeds* (optional)**

*To toast sesame seeds, spread seeds in small skillet. Shake skillet over medium-low heat 3 minutes or until seeds begin to pop and turn golden.

1. Cut eggplant into ½-inch slices; cut each slice into ½×½-inch strips.

2. Heat wok or large nonstick skillet over medium-high heat. Add peanut oil; heat until hot. Add eggplant, garlic and red pepper flakes; stir-fry 7 minutes or until eggplant is very tender and browned.

3. Reduce heat to medium. Add broth, hoisin sauce and green onions to wok; cook and stir 2 minutes. Sprinkle with sesame seeds, if desired.

CASHEW GREEN BEANS

Makes 4 servings

1 tablespoon peanut or vegetable oil

1 small onion, cut into thin wedges

2 cloves garlic, minced

1 package (10 ounces) frozen julienne-cut green beans, thawed, drained and patted dry

2 tablespoons oyster sauce

1 tablespoon rice vinegar

1 tablespoon honey

¼ cup coarsely chopped cashew nuts or peanuts

1. Heat oil in wok or large skillet over medium-high heat. Add onion and garlic; stir-fry 3 minutes.

2. Add green beans; stir-fry 2 minutes. Add oyster sauce, vinegar and honey; stir-fry 1 minute or until heated through. Remove from heat; stir in cashews.

HOT and SOUR ZUCCHINI

Makes 4 servings

2 teaspoons minced fresh ginger

1 clove garlic, minced

¼ teaspoon red pepper flakes or crushed Szechuan peppercorns

1 pound medium zucchini, cut into ¼-inch slices

2 teaspoons sugar

1 teaspoon cornstarch

2 tablespoons red wine vinegar

2 tablespoons soy sauce

1 tablespoon peanut or vegetable oil

1 teaspoon dark sesame oil

1. Combine ginger, garlic and red pepper flakes in medium bowl; mix well. Add zucchini; toss to coat.

2. Combine sugar and cornstarch in small bowl. Stir in vinegar and soy sauce until smooth.

3. Heat large nonstick skillet or wok over medium-high heat. Add peanut oil; heat until hot. Add zucchini mixture; stir-fry 4 to 5 minutes until zucchini is crisp-tender.

4. Stir vinegar mixture; add to skillet. Cook and stir 15 seconds or until sauce boils and thickens. Stir in sesame oil.

WILTED SPINACH MANDARIN

Makes 4 servings

1 tablespoon vegetable oil

½ pound fresh spinach, washed and stemmed

1 cup bean sprouts

1 can (11 ounces) mandarin oranges, drained

2 tablespoons reduced-sodium soy sauce

2 tablespoons orange juice

Quartered orange slices (optional)

1. Heat oil in wok or large skillet over medium-high heat. Add spinach, bean sprouts and mandarin oranges. Stir-fry 1 to 2 minutes just until spinach wilts. Transfer to serving dish.

2. Heat soy sauce and orange juice in wok; pour over spinach, tossing gently to coat. Garnish with orange slices, if desired.

GINGER NOODLES
with SESAME EGG STRIPS

Makes 4 servings

5 egg whites

6 teaspoons teriyaki sauce, divided

3 teaspoons sesame seeds, toasted,* divided

1 teaspoon dark sesame oil

½ cup fat-free reduced-sodium chicken broth

1 tablespoon minced fresh ginger

6 ounces Chinese rice noodles or vermicelli noodles, cooked and well drained

⅓ cup sliced green onions

*To toast sesame seeds, place seeds in small skillet. Shake skillet over medium-low heat 3 minutes or until seeds begin to pop and turn golden.

1. Beat egg whites, 2 teaspoons teriyaki sauce and 1 teaspoon sesame seeds in medium bowl until well blended.

2. Heat oil in large nonstick skillet over medium heat. Pour in egg mixture; cook 1½ to 2 minutes or until bottom is set. Turn over; cook 30 seconds to 1 minute or until cooked through. Gently slide onto plate; cut into ½-inch strips when cool enough to handle.

3. Add broth, ginger and remaining 4 teaspoons teriyaki sauce to skillet; bring to a boil over high heat. Reduce heat to medium; stir in noodles. Cook until heated through. Add omelet strips and green onions; heat through. Sprinkle with remaining 2 teaspoons sesame seeds just before serving.

CHINESE-STYLE FRIED BROWN RICE

Makes 6 servings

3½ cups water

2 cups uncooked long grain brown rice

3 tablespoons vegetable oil, divided

2 eggs, lightly beaten

1 medium yellow onion, coarsely chopped

1 slice (8 ounces) smoked or baked ham, cut into julienne strips

1 cup frozen green peas, thawed

1 to 2 tablespoons soy sauce

1 tablespoon dark sesame oil

Fresh cilantro sprigs (optional)

1. Combine water and rice in large saucepan; cover and bring to a boil over high heat. Reduce heat to low; simmer 40 to 45 minutes or until rice is tender and water is absorbed, stirring occasionally. Remove from heat; let stand, covered, 10 minutes.

2. Fluff rice with fork and spread out on greased baking sheet. Cool to room temperature, about 30 to 40 minutes, or refrigerate overnight.

3. Heat wok over medium heat 30 seconds. Drizzle 1 tablespoon vegetable oil into wok; heat 15 seconds. Add eggs; cook 1 minute or just until set on bottom. Turn eggs over and stir to scramble until cooked but not dry. Remove to small bowl.

4. Add remaining 2 tablespoons vegetable oil to wok; heat over medium-high heat 30 seconds. Add onion; stir-fry about 3 minutes or until tender. Add ham; stir-fry 1 minute. Add cooked rice, peas, soy sauce and sesame oil; cook 5 minutes, stirring frequently. Stir in eggs; cook until heated through. Transfer to warm serving dish; garnish with cilantro.

SWEET ENDINGS

CHINESE ALMOND COOKIES

Makes about 2½ dozen cookies

1 package (about 18 ounces) yellow cake mix

5 tablespoons butter, melted

1 egg

1½ teaspoons almond extract

30 whole almonds

1 egg yolk

1 teaspoon water

1. Beat cake mix, butter, egg and almond extract in large bowl with electric mixer at medium speed until well blended. Shape dough into a disc; wrap and refrigerate 4 hours or overnight.

2. Preheat oven to 350°F. Spray cookie sheets with nonstick cooking spray.

3. Shape dough into 1-inch balls; place 2 inches apart on prepared cookie sheets. Press 1 almond into center of each ball, flattening slightly. Whisk egg yolk and water in small bowl. Brush tops of cookies with egg yolk mixture.

4. Bake 10 to 12 minutes or until lightly browned. Cool on cookie sheets 5 minutes. Remove to wire racks; cool completely.

GOLDEN TREASURE PUDDING

Makes 5 cups

1¾ cups water

1 cup medium-grain rice

2 tablespoons butter

2 cups milk

1 cup coconut milk

⅓ cup sugar

1 to 2 tablespoons diced crystallized ginger

½ cup diced fresh mango, plus additional for garnish

½ cup diced fresh pineapple

Toasted coconut* (optional)

*To toast coconut, spread in single layer in heavy-bottomed skillet. Cook over medium heat 1 to 2 minutes, stirring frequently, until lightly browned. Remove from skillet immediately. Cool before using.

1. Bring water, rice and butter to a boil in medium saucepan. Cover; reduce heat to low. Simmer 15 minutes or until water is absorbed.

2. Stir milk, coconut milk, sugar and ginger into rice mixture. Cook over medium heat, stirring frequently, 15 to 20 minutes or until milk is absorbed and rice is creamy.

3. Stir in ½ cup mango and pineapple. Sprinkle with coconut and additional diced mango, if desired. Serve warm.

FORTUNE COOKIES

Makes 1 dozen cookies

- **2 egg whites**
- **⅓ cup all-purpose flour**
- **⅓ cup sugar**
- **1 tablespoon water**
- **¼ teaspoon vanilla**
- **12 paper fortunes**

1. Preheat oven to 400°F. Spray cookie sheets with nonstick cooking spray.

2. Whisk egg whites in small bowl until foamy. Add flour, sugar, water and vanilla; whisk until smooth.

3. Working in batches of two, place 2 teaspoons batter on prepared cookie sheet for each cookie. Spread batter evenly with back of spoon to 3-inch round. Spray with cooking spray. Bake 4 minutes or until edges are golden brown.

4. Working quickly, remove cookies from cookie sheet and invert onto work surface. Place fortune in centers. Fold cookies in half, pressing on seam. Fold in half again, pressing to hold together. Cool completely.

5. Repeat steps 3 and 4 with remaining batter and fortunes.

ICY MANDARIN DESSERT

Makes 10 servings

½ **gallon vanilla frozen yogurt**

¼ **cup sugar-free maple syrup**

1 **can (11 ounces) mandarin oranges, drained**

½ **cup seedless grapes**

½ **cup toasted pecans,* broken into pieces**

Additional chopped toasted pecans (optional)

*To toast pecans, place in single layer on ungreased baking sheet. Bake in preheated 350°F oven 8 to 10 minutes or until lightly browned, stirring occasionally. Cool before using.

1. Soften frozen yogurt until it resembles thick soup. Place in large loaf pan. Swirl in maple syrup. Fold in oranges, grapes and ½ cup pecans. Freeze until firm.

2. Unmold onto cutting board. Slice and place onto plates when ready to serve. Garnish with additional pecans.

Almond Chicken, 98

METRIC CONVERSION CHART

VOLUME MEASUREMENTS (dry)

$1/8$ teaspoon = 0.5 mL
$1/4$ teaspoon = 1 mL
$1/2$ teaspoon = 2 mL
$3/4$ teaspoon = 4 mL
1 teaspoon = 5 mL
1 tablespoon = 15 mL
2 tablespoons = 30 mL
$1/4$ cup = 60 mL
$1/3$ cup = 75 mL
$1/2$ cup = 125 mL
$2/3$ cup = 150 mL
$3/4$ cup = 175 mL
1 cup = 250 mL
2 cups = 1 pint = 500 mL
3 cups = 750 mL
4 cups = 1 quart = 1 L

VOLUME MEASUREMENTS (fluid)

1 fluid ounce (2 tablespoons) = 30 mL
4 fluid ounces ($1/2$ cup) = 125 mL
8 fluid ounces (1 cup) = 250 mL
12 fluid ounces ($1 1/2$ cups) = 375 mL
16 fluid ounces (2 cups) = 500 mL

WEIGHTS (mass)

$1/2$ ounce = 15 g
1 ounce = 30 g
3 ounces = 90 g
4 ounces = 120 g
8 ounces = 225 g
10 ounces = 285 g
12 ounces = 360 g
16 ounces = 1 pound = 450 g

DIMENSIONS

$1/16$ inch = 2 mm
$1/8$ inch = 3 mm
$1/4$ inch = 6 mm
$1/2$ inch = 1.5 cm
$3/4$ inch = 2 cm
1 inch = 2.5 cm

OVEN TEMPERATURES

250°F = 120°C
275°F = 140°C
300°F = 150°C
325°F = 160°C
350°F = 180°C
375°F = 190°C
400°F = 200°C
425°F = 220°C
450°F = 230°C

BAKING PAN SIZES

Utensil	Size in Inches/Quarts	Metric Volume	Size in Centimeters
Baking or Cake Pan (square or rectangular)	8×8×2	2 L	20×20×5
	9×9×2	2.5 L	23×23×5
	12×8×2	3 L	30×20×5
	13×9×2	3.5 L	33×23×5
Loaf Pan	8×4×3	1.5 L	20×10×7
	9×5×3	2 L	23×13×7
Round Layer Cake Pan	8×1½	1.2 L	20×4
	9×1½	1.5 L	23×4
Pie Plate	8×1¼	750 mL	20×3
	9×1¼	1 L	23×3
Baking Dish or Casserole	1 quart	1 L	—
	1½ quart	1.5 L	—
	2 quart	2 L	—